OPPOSING
VIEWPOINTS®
SERIES

Civil Liberties

Roman Espejo, Book Editor

GREENHAVEN PRESS
A part of Gale, Cengage Learning

GALE
CENGAGE Learning·

Detroit • New York • San Francisco • New Haven, Conn • Waterville, Maine • London

GALE
CENGAGE Learning

Christine Nasso, *Publisher*
Elizabeth Des Chenes, *Managing Editor*

© 2009 Greenhaven Press, a part of Gale, Cengage Learning.

Gale and Greenhaven Press are registered trademarks used herein under license.

For more information, contact:
Greenhaven Press
27500 Drake Rd.
Farmington Hills, MI 48331-3535
Or you can visit our Internet site at gale.cengage.com

For product information and technology assistance, contact us at

Gale Customer Support, 1-800-877-4253
For permission to use material from this text or product, submit all requests online at www.cengage.com/permissions

Further permissions questions can be emailed to permissionrequest@cengage.com

Articles in Greenhaven Press anthologies are often edited for length to meet page requirements. In addition, original titles of these works are changed to clearly present the main thesis and to explicitly indicate the author's opinion. Every effort is made to ensure that Greenhaven Press accurately reflects the original intent of the authors. Every effort has been made to trace the owners of copyrighted material.

Cover photograph reproduced by permission of Glowimages/Getty Images.

LIBRARY OF CONGRESS CATALOGING-IN-PUBLICATION DATA

Civil liberties / Roman Espejo, book editor.
        p. cm. -- (Opposing viewpoints)
    Includes bibliographical references and index.
    ISBN 978-0-7377-4356-2 (hardcover)
    ISBN 978-0-7377-4355-5 (pbk.)
    1. Civil rights--United States--Juvenile literature. 2. Freedom of expression--United States--Junvenile literature. 3. Church and state--United States--Junvenile literature. 4. Privacy, Right of--United States--Junvenile literature. 5. War on Terrorism, 2001---Law and legislation--United States--Junvenile literature. 6. Terrorism--United States--Prevention--Juvenile literature. I. Espejo, Roman, 1977-
    KF4750.C495 2009
    342.7308'5--dc22
                                                    2008054000

Printed in the United States of America
1 2 3 4 5 6 7 13 12 11 10 09

OPPOSING
VIEWPOINTS®
SERIES

| Civil Liberties

Other Books of Related Interest:

Opposing Viewpoints Series

Cyber Crime

At Issue Series

Has Technology Increased Learning?

Current Controversies Series

Domestic Wiretapping

"Congress shall make no law . . . abridging the freedom of speech, or of the press."

First Amendment to the U.S. Constitution

The basic foundation of our democracy is the First Amendment guarantee of freedom of expression. The Opposing Viewpoints Series is dedicated to the concept of this basic freedom and the idea that it is more important to practice it than to enshrine it.

Contents

Chapter 3: Does Technology Threaten Privacy?

Chapter 4: How Has the War on Terrorism Affected Civil Liberties?

Why Consider Opposing Viewpoints?

> *"The only way in which a human being can make some approach to knowing the whole of a subject is by hearing what can be said about it by persons of every variety of opinion and studying all modes in which it can be looked at by every character of mind. No wise man ever acquired his wisdom in any mode but this."*
>
> *John Stuart Mill*

In our media-intensive culture it is not difficult to find differing opinions. Thousands of newspapers and magazines and dozens of radio and television talk shows resound with differing points of view. The difficulty lies in deciding which opinion to agree with and which "experts" seem the most credible. The more inundated we become with differing opinions and claims, the more essential it is to hone critical reading and thinking skills to evaluate these ideas. Opposing Viewpoints books address this problem directly by presenting stimulating debates that can be used to enhance and teach these skills. The varied opinions contained in each book examine many different aspects of a single issue. While examining these conveniently edited opposing views, readers can develop critical thinking skills such as the ability to compare and contrast authors' credibility, facts, argumentation styles, use of persuasive techniques, and other stylistic tools. In short, the Opposing Viewpoints Series is an ideal way to attain the higher-level thinking and reading skills so essential in a culture of diverse and contradictory opinions.

In addition to providing a tool for critical thinking, Opposing Viewpoints books challenge readers to question their own strongly held opinions and assumptions. Most people form their opinions on the basis of upbringing, peer pressure, and personal, cultural, or professional bias. By reading carefully balanced opposing views, readers must directly confront new ideas as well as the opinions of those with whom they disagree. This is not to simplistically argue that everyone who reads opposing views will—or should—change his or her opinion. Instead, the series enhances readers' understanding of their own views by encouraging confrontation with opposing ideas. Careful examination of others' views can lead to the readers' understanding of the logical inconsistencies in their own opinions, perspective on why they hold an opinion, and the consideration of the possibility that their opinion requires further evaluation.

Evaluating Other Opinions

To ensure that this type of examination occurs, Opposing Viewpoints books present all types of opinions. Prominent spokespeople on different sides of each issue as well as well-known professionals from many disciplines challenge the reader. An additional goal of the series is to provide a forum for other, less known, or even unpopular viewpoints. The opinion of an ordinary person who has had to make the decision to cut off life support from a terminally ill relative, for example, may be just as valuable and provide just as much insight as a medical ethicist's professional opinion. The editors have two additional purposes in including these less known views. One, the editors encourage readers to respect others' opinions—even when not enhanced by professional credibility. It is only by reading or listening to and objectively evaluating others' ideas that one can determine whether they are worthy of consideration. Two, the inclusion of such viewpoints encourages the important critical thinking skill of objectively evaluating an author's credentials and bias. This evaluation will illuminate an author's reasons for taking a particular stance on an issue and will aid in readers' evaluation of the author's ideas.

It is our hope that these books will give readers a deeper understanding of the issues debated and an appreciation of the complexity of even seemingly simple issues when good and honest people disagree. This awareness is particularly important in a democratic society such as ours in which people enter into public debate to determine the common good. Those with whom one disagrees should not be regarded as enemies but rather as people whose views deserve careful examination and may shed light on one's own.

Thomas Jefferson once said that "difference of opinion leads to inquiry, and inquiry to truth." Jefferson, a broadly educated man, argued that "if a nation expects to be ignorant and free . . . it expects what never was and never will be." As individuals and as a nation, it is imperative that we consider the opinions of others and examine them with skill and discernment. The Opposing Viewpoints Series is intended to help readers achieve this goal.

David L. Bender and Bruno Leone,
Founders

Introduction

> *"It is now possible to anticipate the closing of Guantánamo, the end to the U.S. practice of executive detention, and the re-affirmation of fundamental human rights principles. . ."*
>
> Manfred Nowak,
> UN Special Rapporteur on torture
> and other cruel, inhuman, or
> degrading treatment or punishment

> *"[Guantánamo] is under attack from human rights groups, civil liberties absolutists, and editorial board armchair generals who have no viable alternative to enemy combatant detention and aggressive interrogation methods to prevent terrorism."*
>
> Michelle Malkin,
> Fox News Channel contributor

During his election campaign for the White House, Barack Obama pledged that he would close the Guantánamo Bay detention camp in Cuba. On August 1, 2007, Obama declared, "As President, I will close Guantánamo, reject the Military Commissions Act, and adhere to the Geneva Conventions." Earlier that May, in Richmond, Virginia, he had described the detention camp as "a sad chapter in American history." At the time, President George W. Bush also aimed to close Guantánamo, but decided against it in October 2008, citing a host of legal and political dangers. His administration was not able to find a country willing to take in Guantánamo detainees, for example.

In November 2008, within a week of Obama's victory in the presidential election, reports surfaced that the president-elect was preparing to move the estimated remaining 250 detainees held at Guantánamo to the United States, where they would be granted constitutional rights and open trials; others cleared for release would be sent home. Meanwhile, civil rights groups called on Obama to immediately fulfill his commitment to shutting down Guantánamo. In a full-page advertisement in the *New York Times*, the American Civil Liberties Union (ACLU) urged him "to fulfill those promises and immediately restore America's moral leadership in the world" on his first day in office.

Guantánamo has served as a U.S. detention center since 2001, holding combatants captured during the war in Afghanistan and suspects in the September 11, 2001, terrorist attacks on the United States. Under the presidency of George W. Bush, detainees linked to al Qaeda and the Taliban were determined to be "enemy combatants"—not affiliated with a national government—thus, ineligible for the full prisoner-of-war (POW) rights established by the Geneva Conventions. This classification has placed the activities at Guantánamo under intense scrutiny and criticism. Complaints of abuses circulated, including torture and religious desecration—most infamously, an incident in which the Qur'an was supposedly flushed in a toilet. Also, a female interrogator purportedly resorted to sexually charged, religiously degrading tactics to "break" a Saudi Arabian who had trained at an American flight school. Other accusations of unusual and brutal interrogation practices at Guantánamo, such as waterboarding, also emerged. Such allegations have been linked to hunger strikes and suicide attempts among detainees.

Critics refute the status of Guantánamo detainees, arguing that the camps—without applying the full protections of the Geneva Conventions—have become a center of unchecked assaults on civil liberties. At her speech for the Amnesty International Report 2005, Irene Khan, the organization's secretary general, argued that Guantánamo "entrench[es] the notion that people can be detained without any recourse to the law," maintaining that more than one hundred unregistered detainees were imprisoned at the detention center. In March 2007, James Yee, a former Muslim chaplain at Guantánamo, contended that "civil liberties are under fire," and the detention center's "secret weapon" is the use of Islam against detainees.

Yet, others suggest that denying Guantánamo detainees the full protections of the Geneva Conventions may not be a clear-cut matter. Thomas Malinowski of Human Rights Watch asks, "What do the conventions tell us about how these prisoners should be treated? The al Qaeda detainees probably are not entitled to formal POW status because they did not fight for a regular army, wear insignia that identified them as soldiers, or respect the rules of war." However, he continues, "Whatever the prisoners' legal status, the Geneva Conventions entitle them to be treated humanely. In many respects, the military has taken this responsibility very seriously. . . ." Article 3 of the Geneva Conventions grants minimal humane treatment to all prisoners of war, regardless of status.

Supporters contend that there are no indications of abuse at the U.S. detention center at all and that its detainees may be worse off if transferred. After evaluating Guantánamo facilities in person and attending interrogations in 2005, Senator Ron Wyden, a Democrat from Oregon, asserted, "I strongly prefer the improved practices and conditions at Camp Delta [in Guantánamo] to the outsourcing of interrogation to countries with a far less significant commitment to human rights." Senator Ben Nelson, a Nebraska Democrat who accompanied Wyden, concurred, "Everything we heard about operations there in the past, we'd have to say, was negative. What we saw firsthand was something different."

The Guantánamo Bay detention center is one of the numerous civil liberties controversies that has resulted from the

U.S.-led war on terror. Related issues, such as racial profiling and federal surveillance, have also given rise to debates surrounding the reach—and limits—of state powers and individual freedoms. *Opposing Viewpoints: Civil Liberties* investigates these and other civil liberties issues in the following chapters: Should Limits Be Placed on Freedom of Expression? Should Church and State Be Separate? Does Technology Threaten Privacy? and How Has the War on Terrorism Affected Civil Liberties? The authors' opinions demonstrate how differing interpretations of fundamental rights lead to contrasting political stances and ideological beliefs.

OPPOSING
VIEWPOINTS®
SERIES

CHAPTER 1

Should Limits Be Placed on Freedom of Expression?

Chapter Preface

On January 5, 2007, the David Ray Hate Crimes Prevention Act, or David's Law, was introduced to the U.S. House of Representatives. The bill seeks to "enhance federal enforcement of hate crimes," including violence based on sexual orientation, by imposing harsher penalties—up to life in prison—for hate crime offenders and providing additional assistance to state and local law enforcement to prosecute hate crimes.

Pending as of November 2008, David's Law is named after David Ray Ritcheson, a Mexican American teenager who gained national attention after surviving a horrific hate crime. On April 23, 2006, at a party in Spring, Texas, the high school freshman was brutally assaulted and taunted with racial epithets by two white males, one a racist skinhead. Ritcheson's injuries were so severe that it required more than thirty surgeries to repair his physical appearance and bodily functions. After months of recovery, Ritcheson testified before the Judiciary Committee in support of the bill on April 17, 2007:

> [T]he hate crime committed against me illustrates that we are still, in some aspects, a house divided. I know now that there are young people in this country who are suffering and confused, thirsting for guidance and in need of a moral compass. These are some of the many reasons I am here before you today asking that our government take the lead in deterring individuals like those who attacked me from committing unthinkable and violent crimes against others because of where they are from, the color of their skin, the God they worship, the person they love, or the way they look, talk, or act.

Ritcheson's testimony is credited with persuading the House of Representatives to pass the Local Law Enforcement Hate Crimes Prevention Act of 2007, a provision of David's

Law. However, the psychological wounds from the attack continued to haunt him. Less than three months later, Ritcheson committed suicide.

In a resolution honoring Ritcheson, Sheila Jackson-Lee, the Democratic representative from Texas who introduced the bill, said, "This tragedy should serve as a wakeup call to the nation of the need to redouble our efforts to prevent hate crimes by juveniles, which I believe is, in the long run, the best and most effective way of eliminating the scourge of hate-motivated crimes from our society." As for Ritcheson's assailants, they were convicted of aggravated assault; one faces life in prison, the other a ninety-year sentence.

Opponents of David's Law, however, contend that it is unconstitutional and would limit free speech. According to Mary Starrett, communications director of the Constitution Party, the bill "would make certain types of speech a federal offense" and "allow federal 'thought police' to interfere in the law enforcement authority of states and localities—something our founders were clear was *not* to be allowed." Others maintain that it would threaten religious freedom. Michael Marcavage, founder and director of the evangelical organization Repent America, argues, "Having been charged under Pennsylvania's hate crimes law for declaring the truth about homosexuality, I can assure you that if this bill is passed and signed into law, it will be used to put Christians behind bars." Moreover, critics allege that David's Law would give special rights to gay and lesbian victims of violent crime. In a 2007 report, political Christian group Concerned Women of America states that this legislation "sends the message that it is more hateful to kill a homosexual than a little child."

Inevitably, David's Law and other hate crime legislation are a flashpoint of political contention. Supporters propose that they protect civil liberties, while detractors claim that such laws criminalize certain types of speech and beliefs. In the following chapter, the authors question whether the freedom of expression has, or should have, limits.

"Free speech does indeed cause hurt— but there is nothing wrong in this."

Free Speech Should Not Be Regulated

Oliver Kamm

In the following viewpoint, Oliver Kamm contends that free speech must be protected because people's feelings cannot be legislated. The author alleges that speech at its most extreme draws attention to social problems and stimulates debate, and moderating speech undermines this process. In fact, Kamm argues that if the state has the power to legislate its citizens' sensibilities, its power is, in effect, limitless. Furthermore, he claims that ideas alone do not merit respect—ideas earn respect through their intellectual resilience. Kamm is an author and columnist for the Times *(UK).*

As you read, consider the following questions:

1. What examples does Kamm give for conflicts between religious faith and freedom of press?
2. How did world leaders react to Ayatollah Khomeini's call for Salman Rushdie's murder, in the author's view?
3. Why does Kamm not defend Holocaust denial?

Oliver Kamm, "The Tyranny of Moderation," *Index on Censorship*, February 2007, pp. 82–86. Reproduced by permission of the publisher, www.indexonline.org.

'The traditional balance between free speech and respect for the feelings of others is evidently becoming harder to sustain,' lamented the columnist and panjandrum Simon Jenkins in the *Sunday Times*. He was writing of the controversy then raging over the publication by the Danish newspaper *Jyllands-Posten* of cartoons lampooning the Prophet Mohammed. 'The best defence of free speech can only be to curb its excess and respect its courtesy,' Jenkins concluded.

A year later, the French satirical magazine *Charlie Hebdo* and its director stood trial, in a case brought by two Muslim organisations, for publicly abusing a group of people because of their religion (*'injure stigmatisant un groupe de personnes à raison de sa religion'*). The magazine had reproduced the offending cartoons and added one of its own for the cover. In March 2007, the court ruled in favour of *Charlie Hebdo* and rejected the Muslim organisations' claim.

Jenkins is the voice of moderation and civility. A declared libertarian, on homosexual law reform to fox hunting, he perceives that a fair society strives to hold values in balance rather than pursue absolutist demands for one at the expense of another. An American equivalent might be the writer K.A. Dilday. Commenting on the *Charlie Hebdo* case on the openDemocracy Web site, she protests that she is 'not a great believer in policing speech'. Yet she does see 'some sense of justice' in such proceedings. They are, after all, effective in stimulating debate and drawing attention to grievance, in a way that France's 'warrior-philosophers' in support of the word do not acknowledge.

Politically Toxic

The voice of moderation, civility, and balance is, in short, politically toxic. It makes the false assumption that having regard to the feelings of others—a virtue in personal affairs—is any concern of public policy. It urgently needs to be rebuffed.

The conflict between religious sensibilities and freedom of publication long predates the Danish cartoons affair. Yet, in British politics and society, the main complainants until the 1990s were orthodox Christians, and their stated concerns were of a general erosion in *mores*. In 1977, Mary Whitehouse, on behalf of her National Viewers' and Listeners' Association, won a famous legal victory in a private prosecution against the newspaper *Gay News*. Her objection was to a poem depicting Christ as a promiscuous homosexual, which she claimed was a blasphemous libel against the Christian faith. Even at the time, the conviction was widely seen as a legal idiosyncrasy and a social anachronism. Had Mrs. Whitehouse couched her claim instead as a complaint about injury to the feelings of Christian believers, she would have had no legal recourse and almost certainly been ignored by mainstream opinion. Yet she would have been anticipating a notion that has in the last two decades become not only common in those same circles but almost axiomatic among some of them.

More than a decade later, Ayatollah Khomeini issued his *fatwa* calling for the murder of a British citizen, Salman Rushdie, for writing a novel. Muslim leaders in the Indian subcontinent had already condemned the book, *The Satanic Verses*, for containing insults to Islam. The *fatwa* made the issue a central one of international politics; and at that point a distinctive claim emerged in western debate.

As in many events of recent British political history, one of the most informative sources—if often unintentionally so—is the voluminous published diaries of former cabinet minister Tony Benn. In his diary entry for 15 February 1989, Benn describes a debate on the Rushdie case held at a meeting of the Campaign Group of left-wing Labour MPs [Members of Parliament]. Some of the responses he records, although cliché-ridden, are recognisably traditional statements of radical politics: 'Mildred Gordon [a former Trotskyite who had become an MP in her 60s] said all fundamentalists and all established churches were enemies of the workers and the people.' But Benn then turns to Bernie Grant, MP for Tottenham, now deceased, who was often wrongly described as among Britain's first black MPs. Benn states: 'Bernie Grant kept interrupting, saying that the whites wanted to impose their values on the world. The House of Commons should not attack other cultures. He didn't agree with the Muslims in Iran, but he supported their right to live their own lives. Burning books was not a big issue for blacks, he maintained.'

The notion that free speech was an ethnocentric imposition on other cultures, to which a properly egalitarian politics would extend respect, has, in a less crude and populist form, developed mightily since. The soft form of that principle is that a culture founded on the free play of ideas needs to exercise restraint in the face of the sensibilities of others. As the Islamic scholar Tariq Ramadan has put it: 'Instead of being obsessed with laws and rights—approaching a tyrannical right to say anything—would it not be more prudent to call upon citizens to exercise their right to freedom of expression responsibly and to take into account the diverse sensitivities that compose our pluralistic contemporary societies?'

Sentiments such as these became established with the Rushdie affair, and have proved an enduring component of our political culture. In 1990, a year after the *fatwa*, Rushdie wrote: 'I feel as if I have been plunged, like Alice, into a world beyond the looking glass, where nonsense is the only available sense. And I wonder if I'll ever be able to climb back through.'

Western political leaders were adept at speaking that form of sense. The first President Bush ventured boldly, a week after the *fatwa* was issued, that the threat of assassination was 'deeply offensive'. The Japanese government anguished and declared: 'Mentioning and encouraging murder is not something to be praised.' The Chief Rabbi in Great Britain, Dr. Imman-

Adult Entertainment and Obscenity

[M]any forms of adult entertainment are referred to as pornography in the common usage. However, the word is frequently misused by those who try to equate "pornography," a word with no legal meaning, with "obscenity," a term which has a legal meaning with specific attributes detailed by the United States Supreme Court in *Miller v. California* (1973).

Obscenity is material deemed by a jury to be outside of the protection of the First Amendment, criminalized by California and most other states as well as in federal law. Pornography, on the other hand, unless it is determined to be obscene in the courts, is *fully protected* by the First Amendment. In fact, *Webster's* dictionary defines pornography as "writings, pictures, etc. intended primarily to arouse sexual desire." By this definition, much of society's poetry, music and other art forms could be described as "pornographic." Henry Miller's *Tropic of Cancer*, James Joyce's *Ulysses* and the film *Carnal Knowledge* and dozens of other literary works, museum exhibits and artworks, as well as adult entertainment products have been accused of being "obscene." Almost all of them have been vindicated in court and restored to the marketplace.

Michelle L. Freridge, "White Paper 2005:
A Report on the Adult Entertainment Industry," 2005.

uel Jakobovits, remarked with ostensible balance but genuine callous stupidity: 'Both Mr. Rushdie and the Ayatollah have abused freedom of speech.'

Surveying these judgments, the writer Jonathan Rauch, in his 1993 book *Kindly Inquisitors* (from which I have taken the quotations), identified a tendency among western intellectuals that would repudiate the sentence but not the notion that Rushdie had committed a crime: 'If we follow this path, then we accept Khomeini's verdict, and we are merely haggling with him over the sentence. If we follow it, then we accept that in principle what is offensive should be suppressed, and we are fighting over what it is . . . that is offensive.'

The Missing Element

This is the missing element in debate over the scope and regulation of speech. The notion that free speech, while important, needs to be held in balance with the avoidance of offence is question-begging, because it assumes that offence is something to be avoided. Free speech does indeed cause hurt—but there is nothing wrong in this. Knowledge advances through the destruction of bad ideas. Mockery and derision are among the most powerful tools in that process. Consider Voltaire's *Candide* or H.L. Mencken's reports—saturated in contempt for religious obscurantists who opposed the teaching of evolution in schools—on the Scopes 'Monkey' Trial.

It is inevitable that those who find their deepest convictions mocked will be offended, and it is possible (though not mandatory, and is incidentally not felt by me) to extend sympathy and compassion to them. But they are not entitled to protection, still less restitution, in the public sphere, even for crass and gross sentiments. A free society does not legislate in the realm of beliefs; by extension, it must not concern itself either with the state of its citizens' sensibilities. If it did, there would in principle be no limit to the powers of the state, even into the private realm of thought and feeling.

The Term "Respect"

The debate has not been aided—it has indeed been severely clouded—by an imprecise use of the term 'respect'. If this is merely a metaphor for the free exercise of religious and political liberty, then it is an unexceptionable principle, but also an unclear and redundant usage. Respect for *ideas* and those who hold them is a different matter altogether. Ideas have no claim on our respect; they earn respect to the extent that they are able to withstand criticism. Even some vocal defenders of liberty stumble on this point. The human rights campaigner Peter Tatchell wrote recently of a particularly slanted television debate: 'Even the supposed Muslim moderates on last night's programme exuded a whiff of hypocrisy. Ibrahim Mogra of the Muslim Council of Britain (MCB) claimed: "We do not wish to impose our way of life on anybody. All we want is to live in respect with one another." Fine sentiments. Shame about the reality.' It is not, in fact, a fine sentiment to require respect. Respect is not an entitlement. It is, at most, a quality that is earned by the intellectual resilience of one's ideas in the public square.

A further complication in the debate is a return—rather an opportunistic one—to the concept of *mores* and its subclass, taboos. In December 2006, the theocratic regime in Iran staged a conference denying the Holocaust, apparently as a retaliatory gesture over the Danish cartoons. I happened to speak in a debate in London the following month with a representative of the Muslim Council of Britain, Inayat Bunglawala, who explicitly treated as analogous the two provocations. There had been 'no need', he said, of the conference. This was entirely to miss the grounds of objection to it. Holocaust denial is wrong not because it is offensive but because it is false. It is a speculative hypothesis that can be consistently maintained only by ignoring or faking historical evidence. There are laws in some European countries against this form of anti-Semitism, and they are misconceived and pernicious for similar reasons to those I have argued. The exposure of Holocaust deniers' claims is the province of competent historians rather than lawyers. The quality of offensiveness is irrelevant to that issue.

Beyond this is a pragmatic question. If those with deeply held convictions find they receive compensation for injured feelings, then mental hurt is what they will seek out. As one group succeeds, then others will perceive the incentive to fashion comparable demands. In Birmingham, [in 2005], protestors forced the closure of a play, *Behzti*, by Gurpreet Kaur Bhatti, which depicted the abuse of Sikh women by Sikh men. With inept jocularity but succinctness, a BBC [British Broadcasting Corporation] correspondent reported: 'If you had to write a theatrical pitch for what Birmingham has just witnessed over the play *Behzti*, you could do it in seven words: play offends community, community protests, play cancelled.'

Campaigners from a pressure group called Christian Voice then, not coincidentally, pressed their own demands. The stage show *Jerry Springer—The Opera* faced protests and threats of prosecution for blasphemy when it was shown on BBC television in 2005 and when it went on tour in 2006. 'I can say with some feeling that the show is crude, offensive and blasphemous in the extreme,' wrote the organisation's director in a letter to theatres urging that they cancel the performances. And, given the precedent, why would he not have issued such a demand?

Trying to make sense of the *Behzti* affair for French readers, the London correspondent of *Libération*, Agnès Poirier, wrote: '*Dans une situation pareille, on attend d'un gouvernement qu'il défende l'auteur menacé.*' [In such a situation, we would expect the government to defend the threatened author.] She noted that the British government minister responsible for community relations, Fiona McTaggart, had in fact done no such thing. Rather, Ms. McTaggart had welcomed the return of calm after the cancellation of the play. Often it takes a detached observer to appreciate fully the corruption of one's own political culture.

This malaise is always a likely outcome of recognising a right to be respected. Respecting the beliefs and feelings of others is a lethal affectation in public policy. It is easy to depict freedom of speech as liable to cause hurt, precisely because it is true. The policy that follows from that is counterintuitive but essential: do nothing. The defence of a free society involves not taking a stand on its output, but insisting on the integrity of its procedures.

> *"The same ideals that justify freedom of speech allow us to determine the limits of that freedom."*

Free Speech Has Limits

Steven J. Heyman

In the following viewpoint, Steven J. Heyman proposes that free speech is an alienable right and is limited by other civil rights. He supports a humanist view of the First Amendment, suggesting that it was originally intended to promote autonomy and democratic self-government while protecting human dignity and equality. According to Heyman, the regulation of free speech is needed to defend individual privacy, security, and reputation. Additionally, the author maintains that some forms of hate speech and pornography are debasing and must be regulated. Heyman is a professor of law at Chicago-Kent College of Law and author of Free Speech and Human Dignity, *from which this viewpoint is excerpted.*

As you read, consider the following questions:

1. In the author's view, what are the "four elements of liberty"?
2. How does Heyman describe the views of free speech in American history?

Steven J. Heyman, *Free Speech and Human Dignity*. New Haven, CT: Yale University Press, 2008. Copyright © 2008 by Steven J. Heyman. All rights reserved. Reproduced by permission.

3. When is expression "wrongful" and subject to regulation, as stated by Heyman?

The First Amendment right to freedom of expression is a defining feature of American society. Yet the scope and meaning of this right have always been controversial. In recent years, much of the debate has focused on issues like hate speech and pornography. Supporters of regulation argue that such speech causes serious injury to individuals and groups and that it assaults their dignity as human beings and citizens. Civil libertarians respond that our commitment to free expression is measured by our willingness to protect it even when it causes serious harm or offends our deepest values. When the issue is framed in this way, we seem to face a tragic choice, one in which we can protect human dignity only by sacrificing freedom of speech, and vice versa. But both of these values are essential to a liberal democratic society. In this way, hate speech and pornography seem to pose an intractable dilemma for the American constitutional order.

Transforming Our Understanding

Moreover, the problem is not confined to those forms of speech but extends to First Amendment jurisprudence as a whole. Contemporary disputes often involve conflicts between free expression and other values. Yet we have no coherent framework that would allow us to determine when speech should receive constitutional protection and when it should be subject to regulation. As a result, controversies over freedom of speech often appear to be irresolvable.

To overcome these difficulties, we must transform our understanding of the First Amendment by developing a theory that is capable of reconciling free speech with other values. . . . Freedom of expression, I shall argue, is founded on respect for the autonomy and dignity of human beings. At the same time, however, this principle also gives rise to other fundamental rights, ranging from personal security and privacy to citizenship and equality. As a general rule, speakers should be required to respect the fundamental rights of others. In this way, the same ideals that justify freedom of speech allow us to determine the limits of that freedom.

[T]his understanding of the First Amendment has deep roots in American constitutional history. Eighteenth-century Americans held that freedom of speech was one of the natural rights of mankind and was essential to republican government. Like all rights, however, free speech was limited by the rights of others. In this way, the concept of rights provided a standard by which to assess regulations of speech. [H]owever, this traditional view no longer prevails. Instead, modern jurisprudence conceives of First Amendment issues not as conflicts of rights, but as conflicts between the individual right to free speech and "social interests" such as dignity and equality. But there is no clear way to resolve clashes between individual rights and social interests. When First Amendment problems are understood in this way, they seem to involve collisions between incommensurable values. That is one reason these disputes have become so bitter and divisive. The best way to escape this predicament is to return to a rights-based theory of the First Amendment.

Four Elements of Liberty

... According to this theory, ... rights are rooted in respect for human beings and their capacity for self-determination. Rights represent what it means for people to be free in various areas of life—not only in relation to the external world, but also in their inner lives, in the social and political realm, and in "the sphere of intellect and spirit." These four elements of liberty correspond to the major justifications that have been advanced for freedom of speech: that it is an aspect of external freedom; that it is essential for individual self-realization; that it is indispensable to democratic self-government; and that it promotes the search for truth. But the same principles that support free speech also support other fundamental rights, including external rights to person and property; personality rights such as privacy and reputation; and rights of citizenship and participation in the society. As I shall explain, the people also have some rights as a community, including the rights to engage in political deliberation and to govern themselves through the democratic process.

On this view, freedom of speech must be exercised with due regard for the rights of other individuals and the community as a whole. Speech that infringes these rights should generally be regarded as wrongful and subject to regulation through narrowly drawn laws. In some cases, however, the value of the speech is so great that it should be protected despite the injury it causes. . . .

[T]his rights-based theory [contrasts] with the Supreme Court's current jurisprudence, which is based on the doctrine of content neutrality. That doctrine holds that "above all else, the First Amendment means that government has no power to restrict expression because of its message, its ideas, its subject matter, or its content." Although this principle captures our strong commitment to freedom of expression, it is fatally one-sided, for it fails to recognize that some kinds of speech (such as defamation and incitement) inflict serious injury precisely because of their content. For this reason, the Court has carved out a series of exceptions to the content-neutrality doctrine. Yet the Justices have never succeeded in explaining the rationale for these exceptions or in squaring them with the general rule. As a result, the Court's First Amendment opinions often seem arbitrary and unpersuasive.

By contrast, I shall argue that the rights-based theory offers a more coherent and principled account of the First Amendment freedom of speech. Of course, I do not mean to say that this theory is capable of generating easy answers to free speech problems. As I have stressed, these problems typically involve important values on both sides. Individuals and groups will often disagree about the relative importance of these values and about how conflicts between them should be resolved. It follows that there will always be ideological disagreement over the scope of free speech. The goal of First Amendment theory should be not to eradicate such disagreement, but to develop a common language or framework within which we can engage in reasoned debate about controversial issues.

For several reasons, I believe that the rights-based theory is best suited to provide such a framework. First, as I have noted, this theory can find strong support in American constitutional history. Second, a belief in rights is deeply embedded in our contemporary political culture. In many cases, the supporters and opponents of regulation are already inclined to state their positions in the language of rights. By the same token, I believe that the principle that freedom of speech is limited by the rights of others is capable of having strong intuitive appeal, not only to the advocates themselves but also to the public at large. Third, the notion of rights plays a pervasive role in American law. Thus, the theory does not require lawyers and judges to use new or unfamiliar concepts, but instead invites them to determine the boundaries of free speech in part by reference to concepts that have been carefully developed in other areas, such as torts, criminal law, and constitutional law. Finally, the theory of rights that I shall develop is based on the idea of mutual recognition and respect: rights instantiate the respect that individuals owe one another as human beings and citizens. Understood in this manner, the idea of rights may offer a way to overcome the deep divisions and mistrust that mark current debates over freedom of expression.

Liberal and Humanist

[T]he rights-based theory [applies] to a wide range of First Amendment controversies. In accord with the civil libertarian tradition . . . the Constitution should afford strong protection

What Counts as Speech?

Given our very substantial commitment to free speech, it is crucial that we be as clear as possible about what that commitment involves. Despite this, there is (at least) one important source of confusion here, namely, what counts as speech in such contexts. It is generally agreed that our commitment to free speech entails extending to speech special protections that we don't extend to other actions. But there is less agreement regarding the following question: how should the term 'speech' be understood here? Is the term being used in its ordinary sense, or in some special technical sense? If the latter, what is this special technical sense? In other words, insofar as the First Amendment enshrines the right to free speech, which actions should be taken to fall within the scope of that amendment?

Ishani Maitra and Mary Kate McGowan,
"The Limits of Free Speech: Pornography, Hate Speech,
and the Question of Coverage," 2005. http://web.syr.edu.

to revolutionary speech, flag burning, and other forms of expression that criticize the government or the existing political order. By contrast, I believe that the state should have greater authority to regulate speech that is directed against individuals or groups. [S]ome forms of expression—such as incitement, threats, and fighting words—should be denied constitutional protection because they infringe the fundamental right to personal security or freedom from violence. I argue that the state should also be allowed to protect the right to privacy against unreasonable intrusion or exposure. I then apply this view to a variety of contemporary problems, including sidewalk counseling at abortion clinics, protests at military funerals, and news reports that reveal the identity of rape victims. Finally, . . . I contend that some forms of hate speech and pornography can be regulated on the ground that they violate the most basic right of all—the right to recognition as a human being and a member of the community.

In short, . . . freedom of expression should be understood within a broader conception of rights based on human dignity and autonomy. This view recognizes a strong, liberal right to freedom of expression, at the same time that it affords protection against the most serious forms of "assaultive speech." In this way, it seeks to develop some common ground between civil libertarianism and its critics.

The view I present may also be called a liberal humanist theory of the First Amendment. It is liberal in its emphasis on the protection of individual rights; it is humanist in holding that those rights are founded on respect for the intrinsic worth of human beings and are meant to enable them to develop their nature to the fullest extent. I believe that a theory of this sort offers the best hope of reconciling our competing commitments to human dignity and freedom of speech. . . .

The Scope and Limits of Freedom of Speech

At the core of the rights-based theory are two principles which emerged from my account of the natural rights background of the First and Fourteenth Amendments. First, freedom of speech is an inherent right that belongs to individuals both as human beings and as citizens in a democratic society. Second, like all rights, free speech may be regulated to protect the rights of others.

[A]lthough these two principles were once widely accepted, they fell into disfavor in the late nineteenth and early twentieth centuries. In recent times, the idea that individuals have an inherent right to free speech has once more gained currency. By contrast, the idea that this freedom is limited by the rights of others no longer plays a major role in First Amendment jurisprudence. Nevertheless, one can still find traces of this idea in the Supreme Court's opinions. This is true even of the dissent in *Abrams v. United States* (1919), which helped give birth to the modern view. In that case, Justices [Oliver Wendell] Holmes and [Louis] Brandeis argued that the First Amendment should protect political expression except in the most extraordinary circumstances. At the same time, they implied that a different standard should apply "where private rights are . . . concerned." Similarly, in *West Virginia State Board of Education v. Barnette* (1943), which held that public school children could not be compelled to salute the flag, Justice [Robert H.] Jackson observed that "[t]he freedom asserted by these [individuals] does not bring them into collision with rights asserted by any other individual. It is such conflicts which most frequently require intervention of the State to determine where the rights of one end and those of another begin." In recent decades, the Justices have occasionally described particular issues as conflicts between free speech and other rights such as reputation, privacy, and the constitutional guarantee of a fair trial. In some cases, they have even perceived conflicts between different First Amendment values. Moreover, even when the Justices use the language of competing interests, they may analyze issues in a way that resembles a balancing of rights.

Although these cases do not represent the dominant position in contemporary First Amendment jurisprudence, they do offer some doctrinal support for the principle I wish to establish: that freedom of speech must be exercised with due regard for the rights of others. This principle is also accepted within the broader human rights tradition. For example, it appears in such documents as the International Covenant on Civil and Political Rights and the European Convention on Human Rights, both of which hold that expression is a fundamental freedom which is subject to restriction on certain grounds, including where necessary to protect the rights or reputations of others.

Against this background, we can now formulate a basic model of the scope and limits of the First Amendment freedom of speech. On the liberal humanist view, free speech generally should be considered a fundamental right. At the same time, that right is bounded by the rights of other individuals and the community. More specifically, an act of expression should be regarded as presumptively wrongful and subject to legal regulation when it (1) causes or is otherwise responsible for (2) an infringement of a fundamental right belonging to another, and (3) the actor has a level of fault that should make her responsible for that result. Speech can cause injury to other rights either directly (as when *A* threatens *B*) or indirectly (as when *A* incites *B* to attack *C*). To ensure broad protection for free speech, an act of expression should not be deemed to cause the infringement of another right unless it has a concrete and substantial impact on that right. The precise scope of responsibility will vary, however, depending on such factors as the nature and value of the competing rights and the type of sanctions at issue (for example, criminal punishment or civil liability). Similar factors are relevant in determining the appropriate standard of fault. In many cases, individuals should be held responsible only when they intentionally violate the rights of others. Other situations may call for a different standard, such as recklessness or negligence.

Important Qualifications

The principle that free speech is limited by the rights of others is subject to several important qualifications. First, . . . there are situations in which the value of the expression is so great that it should be protected despite its impact on other rights. A classic example is *New York Times Co. v. Sullivan* (1964), in which the Supreme Court held that the right to criticize the conduct of public officials is so important for democratic self-governance that the speech should generally be protected, even if it turns out to be false and damaging to an official's reputation.

Second, in its effort to do justice, the law must take account not only of what is right in itself, but also of the law's own nature and limitations. For instance, the state cannot properly regulate speech (or any other form of activity) unless it is able to draw the line between lawful and unlawful action in reasonably clear terms that are capable of being understood by those who must administer or comply with the law. This is the basis of the constitutional doctrines of vagueness and overbreadth, which play an especially prominent role in First Amendment jurisprudence. Regulation is also inappropriate if it is likely to do more harm than good from the standpoint of constitutional liberty. Again, government should have less authority to regulate in contexts where it is likely to be biased in favor of restriction. I shall refer to considerations of this sort as those of institutional right. In some cases, those concerns will justify according speech more (or less) protection than it is entitled to as a matter of substantive right. This course should be followed, however, only where necessary to make the law more consistent with right as a whole.

Third, in arguing that freedom of speech is limited by other rights, I do not mean to deny that some speech is properly subject to broader regulation. [C]lassical natural rights theory held that some aspects of liberty were inalienable while others were alienable. Inalienable rights were limited solely by the rights of others, while alienable rights were also subject to regulation for the public good. Similarly, modern constitutional law distinguishes between fundamental rights, which can be restricted only for compelling reasons, and nonfundamental rights, which are subject to reasonable regulation to promote social welfare. Although freedom of speech generally should be regarded as a fundamental right, that is not true of all sorts of speech. For example, I am inclined to think that commercial advertising, like other forms of business activity, should be considered a nonfundamental right subject to reasonable regulation. For the most part, however, I shall not pursue such issues in this book but shall focus instead on the limits that arise from the rights of others and that apply to all forms of expression.

Finally, my claim that free speech may be restricted solely to protect the rights of others is meant to apply only to regulations that are based on the content or "communicative impact" of expression—that is, on what the speaker was saying or the effect it might have on others. The extent to which the government may impose other kinds of regulations (such as those that are limited to the time, place, and manner of speech) is a separate issue.

> *"Even if Hate Speech does have a social value in reaffirming belief in equality of the races, it seems that the social harm far outweighs the good."*

Hate Speech Should Be Regulated

Liam Martin

In the following viewpoint, Liam Martin maintains that constitutional protection should not be extended to hate speech. Drawing upon landmark court cases in the United States, the author argues that the potential of hate speech to provide falsities, obstruct justice, and incite violence defeats its little, if any, social value. But Martin advises that such a restriction depends on the context in which hate speech is delivered. Therefore, he concludes that speech that is racially libelous or threatens national security must be restricted by the state and consistently penalized by the courts. Martin is a 2006 Harvard graduate with a degree in government.

As you read, consider the following questions:

1. According to Martin, what is John Stuart Mill's position on "free expression"?

Liam Martin, "Hate Speech: Free Expression or Clear and Present Danger?" *American Chronicle*, June 23, 2007. Reproduced by permission of author.

2. How does the author define group libel?

3. In Martin's view, what does the corn-dealer example demonstrate?

The nineteenth-century British utilitarian, John Stuart Mill, recognized and advocated the importance of free speech. In his work, *On Liberty*, Mill contended that it is essential to the well-being of society and the discovery of truth that speech be virtually unregulated by the state. Adopting this approach, the framers of the U.S. Constitution included within the First Amendment the Free Speech Clause, declaring, "Congress shall make no law . . . abridging the freedom of speech." The freedom this stipulation granted has proven to be quite complicated in practice. The Supreme Court, for one, has continually struggled with cases involving speech that allegedly poses a threat to security. Through an examination of two specific case-areas on which the Court has ruled, Hate Speech and the Clear and Present Danger Doctrine, it becomes clear that while expression is important, so too is a recognition of the costs it inflicts on society. While the Court recognized through the Clear and Present Danger Doctrine the need for this balance and rightly restricted speech, it failed to recognize similar dangers inherent in Hate Speech. Even Mill argued that certain expressions could legitimately be regulated by the state; Hate Speech and those types of speech which are clearly and presently dangerous fall into this category.

Mill on "Free Expression"

It is important to clarify Mill's case for the benefits of free speech. According to Mill, state regulation of speech would hinder the discovery of truth and thus the progress of mankind in two ways. First, the suppression of opinion could result in the suppression of truth: "the opinion which it is attempted to suppress by authority may possibly be true." After all, notes Mill, "the fact of [mankind's] fallibility" makes certainty of any belief impossible; there thus ought to be a readiness to accept the expression of opinions, as they may very well shed light on new truths before thought to be falsities. Second, even if the aforementioned opinion is false, it is healthy for the truth to be challenged by opposing views. By challenging truth, even with falsities, one strengthens belief therein. Truth and falsity, therefore, should be expressed, both because the discernment of truth and falsity is difficult, and because truth is most widely acknowledged when challenged by falsity.

However, under the Harm Principle, Mill argues that expression can be limited when it inflicts harm on others: "even opinions lose their immunity, when the circumstances in which they are expressed are such as to constitute their expression a positive instigation to some mischievous act. . . . Acts . . . which, without justifiable cause, do harm to others, may be . . . controlled . . . by the active interference of mankind." Thus it is that the Harm Principle of Mill's theory does indeed limit speech to an arena in which speech does not "instigate" harm to others.

Hate Speech—the Court's Approach

Hate Speech, as defined by [late constitutional law scholar] Gerald Gunther, is speech that is "perceived as harmful and offensive to racial or religious minorities or other historically disempowered groups." Historically, as long as this speech is not accompanied by hate crimes, the Supreme Court has allowed it, arguing that the importance of free speech in cases of Hate Speech outweighs any harm inflicted upon the group or society at large.

In 1978, the community of Skokie, Illinois, with a large population of Jews, enacted three ordinances in an attempt to ban the National Socialist Party (Nazi demonstrators) from marching publicly in their city square. Two of these ordinances attempted indirect obstruction through insurance requirements and dress codes; the third effectively forbade Hate Speech by prohibiting the "dissemination of any materials within [Skokie] which [intentionally] promotes and incites hatred against persons by reasons of their race, national origin, or religion." The Court declared in *National Socialist Party v. Skokie* that these ordinances were unconstitutional, contending that the harm of Hate Speech was bearable given the greater harm inflicted by an overly-involved and regulatory government: "it is better to allow those who preach racial hate to expend their venom in rhetoric rather than to be panicked into embarking on the dangerous course of permitting the government to decide what its citizens may say and hear." The Court reaffirmed this holding in *R.A.V. v. St. Paul*, ruling that a Minnesotan ordinance forbidding the placement of a "burning cross or Nazi swastika" on public or private property was unconstitutional on the grounds that it limited speech based on its content or viewpoint. Thus it was, through *Skokie* and *St. Paul*, that the Court established a general acceptance of Hate Speech.

Hate Speech—Conceptualizing Free Speech

Using a number of additional cases considered by the Court, further details of *Skokie* and *St. Paul*, and even Millean theory, it becomes clear that the harm done to society by hate speech warrants state action against it, in spite of free speech concerns. According to Mill, speech should be protected both because it might be true and, if false, will strengthen belief in truth. Taking these two benefits into consideration, one can see that Hate Speech provides neither. First, even if claims under Hate Speech (such as the Nazis' claim that Jews are inferior) could not be proven false empirically, it would seem a crime against equality for the state not to adopt the position that they were nevertheless false. On certain issues, such as science, the state should be required to allow alternative theories as it has been demonstrated in the past that new truths will emerge through such discussion. However, it is unlikely that any new truths will be learned about the inferiority of Jews; and if such evidence did emerge, what benefit could it provide to the society? On the contrary, such evidence would lead to the further persecution of Jews, a result which is hardly beneficial to the community, regardless of verifiability. Truth is not an end unto itself; truth which justifies further discrimination is, for instance, of no value to society. Because Hate Speech, even if true, would be more harmful than helpful, it provides no benefits of the new truth described by Mill as desirable and thus can be regulated by the state.

Second, if false (as is likely the case), Hate Speech is far more detrimental to society than it is complementary to truth. According to Mill, falsity is valuable because it demonstrates the strength of truth. However, it seems that neither hate-speakers nor hearers will experience this benefit. First, from the speaker's perspective, it seems unlikely that the Nazis planning demonstrations in Skokie or those burning crosses in St. Paul will reverse their opinions on race through the free expression of their beliefs; and from the hearer's perspective, the belief in racial equality is firm and claims against it will thus in no way serve to reaffirm. Moreover, even if Hate Speech does have a social value in reaffirming belief in equality of the races, it seems that the social harm far outweighs the good. This claim can be corroborated by the following two points:

1) Group Libel: Despite its decisions in *Skokie* and *St. Paul*, the Court ruled against Hate Speech in *Beauharnais v. Illinois*. In this case, the Court upheld an Illinois law prohibiting the public distribution "of any publication which 'portrays depravity, criminality, unchastity, or lack of virtue of a class of citizens, of any race, color, creed or religion.'" By this decision, the Court admitted that hate-speakers can be viewed as "purveyors of falsehood"; more important, the Court did not protect the right to express this "falsehood." Why? Because Hate Speech in this case could have "a powerful emotional impact

on those to whom it was presented," and thus "obstructs the manifold adjustments required for free" life in a democracy. Indeed, blacks exposed to the burning of a cross in their neighborhood, as discussed in St. Paul, might begin to feel unequal. The Court demonstrated in *Brown v. Board of Education* that certain messages, even if no actual inequality is imposed upon members of a race, can lead to feelings of inferiority. Hate Speech, like segregation, sends a message to its targets, especially children, which can affect their perceptions and create inferiority complexes. It seems more important to prevent this effect, as the Court recognized in *Beauharnais*, than it is to allow for the expression of hateful opinions.

2) Fighting Words: Even Mill was quick to qualify the freedom of expression when it threatened to harm others: "An opinion that corn-dealers are starvers of the poor . . . may justly incur punishment when delivered orally to an excited mob assembled before the house of a corn-dealer." In a decision reminiscent of this standard, the Court upheld in *Chaplinsky v. New Hampshire* a law "stating that no person 'shall address any offensive, derisive, or annoying word to any other person,'" and claimed that certain types of speech justify state intervention; "these include . . . 'fighting words—those which by their very utterance inflict injury or tend to incite an immediate breach of the peace." This almost perfectly describes the nature of Hate Speech. Is the Nazis' claim of Jewish inferiority not offensive, derisive, or annoying; does it not inflict injury or invite violence? Indeed, considering that Skokie had a large population of Jews, many of whom were survivors of Nazi persecution, it is highly likely that a violent situation could arise. As such, it seems reasonable to argue that the threat posed by Hate Speech justifies its categorization as "fighting words," and to thus regulate it.

John Stuart Mill recognized the dangers of free speech, and argued that limitations were necessary in certain cases. From the perspective of his list of benefits to the expression of opinion, Hate Speech fails on all counts: it can provide no beneficial truth; it might provide falsities, but these seem to have little value or value that is far outweighed by the subsequent costs of inequality and violence.

Despite these arguments, the Supreme Court established, through the cases of *Skokie* and *St. Paul,* a general leniency towards Hate Speech, failing to recognize its categorization either as "Group Libel" or "Fighting Words." Instead, it ascribed to Hate Speech a social value through the First Amendment which it seems even Mill would have rejected. In this series of cases, therefore, it seems that the Court decided incorrectly.

Clear and Present Danger— the Court's Approach

Unlike in the Hate Speech cases, the Supreme Court was far quicker, through the Clear and Present Danger Doctrine, to limit speech which posed a threat to the security of the state or society. Through the corn-dealer example, Mill recognized that the "circumstances in which [opinions] are expressed" are of paramount importance and should be considered when determining the state's right to interfere with speech. It is this principle which the Court adopted through the Clear and Present Danger Doctrine, initiated and widely prescribed during World War I.

Fearful of spy activity and the disruption of war-time efforts, the government enacted the 1917 Espionage Act, making illegal interference in the state's efforts in the War, including disruption of military or naval operations, causation of disloyalty or mutiny, or obstruction of military recruiting services. Following the establishment of this law, the Court faced a number of cases involving such interferences. In general, the Court ruled in favor of the interests of the state and against the interests of free speech, citing throughout the Clear and Present Danger Doctrine.

The Physical Harms of Hate Speech

Hate speech is not merely unpleasant or offensive. It may leave physical impacts on those it visits, particularly when uttered in one-on-one situations accompanied by at least an implicit threat—that is, by someone taller, larger, or more powerful than the victim or in a position of authority vis-à-vis him or her. The same is true when the hate speaker is a member of a group engaged in taunting a single member of a disempowered minority faction. Then, the response is internalized, as it must be, for talking back will be futile or even dangerous. In fact, many hate crimes have taken place when the victim did just that—spoke back to the aggressor and paid with his or her life.

The immediate, short-term harms of hate speech include rapid breathing, headaches, raised blood pressure, dizziness, rapid pulse rate, drug-taking, risk-taking behavior, and even suicide. The stresses of repeated racial abuse may have long-term consequences, including damaged self-image, lower aspiration level, and depression.

Richard Delgado and Jean Stefancic,
Understanding Words That Wound.
Boulder, CO: Westview Press, 2004.

Schenck v. United States, the opinion of which was delivered by Justice [Oliver Wendell] Holmes, constituted the Court's first statement and application of this standard. In a passage reminiscent of Mill's corn-dealer example, Holmes declared that "the character of every act depends upon the circumstances in which it is done. . . . [The] question in every case is whether the words used are used in such circumstances and are of such a nature as to create a clear and present danger." In other words, speech is generally free, but must be limited and indeed forbidden when it places the society in danger. This is a clear example of state interest weighed against the interest of free speech. The Court reaffirmed this principle in two subsequent cases, *Frohwerk v. United States* and *Debs v. United States*, upholding the convictions of a German publicist who ran a newspaper which attempted to undermine U.S. war efforts, and a Socialist presidential candidate who incited a group of demonstrators against the activities of the United States in Germany. In these three cases, the state interest is considered by the Court to be paramount, and speech is thereby restricted.

Clear and Present Danger—Conceptualizing Free Speech

Having thus noted the Court's claim to the state's interest in upholding the restrictions of the 1917 Espionage Act through *Schenck, Frohwerk, Debs,* and *Abrams* [*v. United States* (1919)], it is important, as with Hate Speech, to determine the interests of free speech as it applies to these cases. Turning back to Mill, one considers again the two possible ways in which the expression of opinion can be valuable to society: the opinion may shed light on a new truth and the opinion, if not true, adds strength to the truth it opposes on false grounds. This distinction of true/false, however, does not apply to the speech exercised in the above cases. The defendants made general, opinionated statements about the morality of the War, capitalism, and the American government. Unlike in the Hate Speech cases, where certain statements made by the defendants are simply false (such as the statement that Jews are inferior), these cases do not involve such statements of fact and thus do not fall into the true/false categorization. This is exactly why, Mill would say, speech against the government, or capitalism, or the like, should be allowed; because human fallibility, along with the nature of these opinions, prevents the state from knowing with certainty the veracity of such statements and thus requires that all opinions be heard so as to discover the one which works best for the community. It would seem then that, under this logic, the state overstepped its bounds in regulating the speech involved in the clear and present danger cases.

However, to make this claim would be both to misunderstand Millean free speech and to underestimate the government's interest in protecting itself. First, Mill himself recognized that the extent of the liberty of speech depended upon circumstances. Again, Mill's classic corn-dealer example makes it clear that speech in certain contexts can be limited by the government for the protection of individuals and the society at large. In the clear and present danger cases, the Court determined that the circumstances, namely World War I, were such that restrictions must be placed on certain types of speech, in certain forums, so as to protect the state's interests.

Second, the Court is only limiting those types of speech it addresses in the WWI cases within certain contexts. [Union leader and political activist] Eugene Debs, for instance, is free to advocate Socialism and criticize the war to friends, family, and even small crowds. His speech became illegal when it entered into the context of thousands of angry protesters who were already somewhat of a threat and now were being incited. [German newspaper editor Jacob] Frohwerk can publish articles criticizing the war and the American government; it just cannot do so in locations where that speech might incite obstruction of American war efforts. In other words, the struggle for truth with which Mill is so concerned can still occur under the clear and present danger decisions; it is simply limited to an extent based on the context of the struggle. Third, it is important to recognize that certain speech constitutes action. In the famous [Judge] Learned Hand decision in

Masses Publishing Co. v. Patten, Hand notes that expression which "counsels" others to mutinous or insubordinate action against the government is itself action towards that cause. "One may not counsel or advise others to violate the law as it stands. Words are not only the keys of persuasion, but the triggers of action, and those which have no purport but to counsel the violation of law cannot by any latitude of interpretation be a part of that public opinion which is the final source of government in a democratic state." As such, these "triggers of action," considered here as devoid of value as "public opinion," are treatable as action themselves, and are thus more legitimately regulated by the government. Even Mill argues that "No one pretends that actions should be as free as opinions." From these three points, it can be summarized that speech of the kind addressed in the clear and present danger cases is, under Mill's standards and the standards of protection necessary to a state, justifiably restricted.

Having considered first the state's interests in regulating speech in the WWI cases, and second the interests of expression of the kind addressed in these same cases, it seems evident that the interests of the state outweigh those weaker interests of free speech declared by the defendants. The Court, unlike in the Hate Speech cases, recognized this balance and ruled rightly by its adoption of the Clear and Present Danger Doctrine.

As Justice Holmes declared, the circumstances and nature of every speech must be considered when determining the freedom thereof. In WWI, the Court, sensitive to this need by virtue of the grave situation facing the country, was quick to protect the interests of the state and society. It was indeed right to do so. However, it failed to strike this same balance in the equally grave and dangerous context of America's history of race relations. Given this context, it is vital to the interests of peace, equality, and the integrity of the American mind and spirit that speech which libelously offends groups especially on the basis of race or ethnicity, as well as speech which threatens the security of the country, be limited by the state. The Court must be more consistent in defending this need, and hopefully will be so in the future.

"The implementation of hate speech legislation, particularly in the religious sphere, has resulted in serious issues of free speech restriction and violation of religious rights."

Hate Speech Should Not Be Regulated

Jonathan Gallagher

According to Jonathan Gallagher in the following viewpoint, legislation intended to restrict so-called "hate speech"—religious beliefs, moral views, and creative expression—infringes on human rights. For instance, he asserts that individuals who openly disapprove of homosexuality on the basis of their religious convictions have been unfairly convicted of "hate speech," which criminalizes personal conviction and oversteps religious freedom. Gallagher insists that these measures are counterproductive and can give rise to an atmosphere of silenced dissent, limited debate, and religious intolerance and persecution. Gallagher is deputy secretary general of the International Religious Liberty Association, a religious freedom advocacy organization based in Washington, DC.

Jonathan Gallagher, "When Speech Becomes Dangerous," *Liberty Magazine*, May-June 2008. Reproduced by permission.

As you read, consider the following questions:

1. As noted by the author, why have Catholic adoption agencies been closed down?
2. In Gallagher's view, how did the United Nations (UN) deal with the Danish cartoon controversy?
3. How does Gallagher allude to George Orwell to support his viewpoint?

"Seven years jail for gay hate preachers," announced Britain's *Telegraph* newspaper on October 9, 2007, reporting government plans to introduce new hate speech legislation to the U.K. Parliament. This follows on from new "religious hatred" legislation, already passed, that became law a week previous.

One response to this new proposal came from an intriguing source—the English comedian Rowan Atkinson who plays the role of "Mr. Bean." (Having once stood in the middle of Hong Kong Airport watching this very visual humor [no sound necessary] I can personally testify that at least a dozen different nationalities present were finding him very funny.)

So it's a little strange that a comic should be writing to *The Times* (of London) to protest such heavyweight issues, perhaps. In his letter, Atkinson makes the telling point that even those in the presumed victimized minority do not see the need for such legislation, and that the proposals end up in a sadly futile exercise to legislate what is far more of a social than a legal problem. Even worse, says Atkinson, is the detrimental effects on freedom of speech. He ends his letter like this:

"This 'tick the box if you'd like a law to stop people being rude about you' is one way of filling the legislative program, but there are serious implications for freedom of speech, humor, and creative expression.

"The devil, as always, will be in the detail, but the casual ease with which some people move from finding something offensive to wishing to declare it criminal—and are then able to find factions within government to aid their ambitions—is truly depressing." This comes in the same week as U.K. news reports that:

Catholic adoption agencies are having to close down their operations rather than follow government demands that they agree to place children with homosexuals.

A very successful foster couple who have looked after 28 children are now being forced to resign because they refuse to sign that they will promote homosexuality as valid to children as young as 11, which is in complete conflict with their Christian beliefs.

A magistrate felt obliged to resign from his post because he was refused permission to opt out of decisions to place adopted children with same-sex parents.

Criminalizing Beliefs

Some may take such news reports as proof that compelling people to act against their religious beliefs is absolutely necessary. Others may see such actions as heavy-handed government interference in people's personal convictions. Whether any attitude is offensive is very dependent on the perspective of both parties—the offender and the offendee. Most disturbing is the desire to criminalize beliefs, offensive or otherwise, as Atkinson observed.

So will it really be "Seven years jail for gay hate preachers"? In a desire to be nondiscriminatory, equal, and nonoffensive, a number of countries have passed legislation to combat what they identify as "hate speech." The results have hardly been inspiring.

The case of Ake Green, a Pentecostal pastor in Sweden, has received much coverage. He was convicted of hate speech against homosexuals. The prosecutor in the case is reported as saying: "One may have whatever religion one wishes, but this is an attack on all fronts against homosexuals. Collecting Bible citations on this topic as he does makes this hate speech."

While it may be that the sermon went beyond simply a recitation of Bible texts, and while there are other aspects to this case that deserve attention, it is true that Pastor Green did receive a prison sentence before the case was overturned on appeal by the Swedish Supreme Court.

A Canadian case parallels that of Green. In 1997 Hugh Owens of Regina, Saskatchewan, Canada, placed an ad in a local newspaper with four Bible verses condemning homosexuality, together with a sign indicating homosexuality was not allowed. He was tried and convicted, together with the newspaper, of breaching the Saskatchewan Human Rights Code, and ordered to pay damages. In the first appeal, which was denied, Justice J. Barclay in his judgment observed in connection with Leviticus 20:13 that "the biblical passage which suggests that if a man lies with a man they must be put to death exposes homosexuals to hatred."

Owens won on appeal to the Saskatchewan Court of Appeal, which said the ad did not contravene the code.

What both cases do reveal is that some, including those within the judiciary, do believe that quoting the Bible on homosexuality is indeed hate speech.

Commenting on the case, Janet Epp Buckingham, director of Law and Public Policy and general legal counsel for the Evangelical Fellowship of Canada in Ottawa, wrote:

"I, for one, do not believe it is particularly Christian to go around condemning people and then claim that it is part of one's religious beliefs. Nevertheless, once an issue like this gets to court, and the courts start dealing with religious freedom, Christians need to be there to ensure that Christians do not lose the ability to distribute Scriptures or the ability to speak publicly on sexual morality as a side casualty in the legal process. At the Saskatchewan Queen's Bench, the judge ruled that Leviticus 20:13 promotes hatred against gays."

Hate Speech on the Global Scene

So what of the wider aspects of religious free speech that can be regarded as hate speech? Various countries are considering, or have already adopted, hate speech legislation that includes religious hate speech, with some exclusions based on religious conviction. The United Nations [UN] has been occupied (some might even say preoccupied) with such issues, especially since the Danish cartoon controversy. As a result, various proposals to deal with "defamation" (UN-speak for hate speech) have been floated, particularly at the UN Human Rights Council in Geneva. The latest round has seen defenders of religious liberty and freedom of expression in conflict with such organizations as the Organization of the Islamic Conference (OIC), and even the Human Rights Council (which as currently composed has a majority of Muslim countries).

Asked to prepare materials dealing with the issue of defamation, UN special rapporteurs Doudou Diene and Asma Jahangir have made clear the position that while not defending incitement to religious hatred, no religion or believer can expect to be free from criticism.

"... International human rights law protects primarily individuals in the exercise of their freedom of religion and not religions per se. . . . The right to freedom of religion or belief, as enshrined in relevant international legal standards, does not include the right to have a religion or belief that is free from criticism or ridicule. . . . Defamation of religions may offend people and hurt their religious feelings, but it does not necessarily, or at least directly, result in a violation of their rights, including their right to freedom of religion. Freedom of religion primarily confers a right to act in accordance with one's religion but does not bestow a right for believers to have their religion itself protected from all adverse comment."

In fact, hate speech legislation relative to religion can be seriously counterproductive, they note.

The Opposite Effect

Empowering the State to proscribe and punish speech is not only the most dangerous step a society can take—though it is that—it's also the most senseless. It never achieves its intended effect of suppressing or eliminating a particular view. If anything, it has the opposite effect, by driving it underground, thus preventing debate and exposure. Worse, it converts its advocates into martyrs ... who now become self-glorifying symbols of individual liberty rather than what they are: hateful purveyors of a bitter, destructive, authoritarian ideology.

Glen Greenwald, "The Noxious Fruits of Hate Speech Laws,"
Salon, January 13, 2008. www.salon.com.

"In a number of states, in all regions of the world and with different religious backgrounds, some forms of defamation of religion constitute a criminal offense. While the different responses to such defamations depend on various factors, including historical and political factors, criminalizing defamation of religion can be counterproductive. The rigorous protection of religions as such may create an atmosphere of intolerance and can give rise to fear and may even provoke the chances of a backlash. There are numerous examples of persecution of religious minorities as a result of excessive legislation on religious offenses or overzealous application of laws that are fairly neutral. As a limit to freedom of expression and information, it can also limit scholarship on religious issues and may asphyxiate honest debate or research."

Speaking in New York on October 25, 2007, shortly before her detention under house arrest in Pakistan, Jahangir observed that "objective criticism of religion is a human right," and that "defamation is sometimes stretched to include criticism. If some definitions of defamation are adopted, social norms based on religion could not be debated. Defamation is an issue of civil law, not a violation of human rights." She also critiqued blasphemy laws that are used to silence dissent.

Religion and race are sometimes compared to each other, she said, and then the provisions against racial hatred are applied to religion. But, she observed, "religion is unlike race—you cannot proselytize to change one's race. There are serious differences." [She also noted,] "Additionally, there is not a consensus among states on fundamental issues, such as conversion. Some are not willing to accept the idea of leaving a faith community." So, how best to deal with true religious hatred, rather than objective criticism (though, as already noted, much depends on the individual perspective)? Jahangir again:

"It is my firm belief that religious hatred can best be combated by sound policies and by building strong public opinion against it. However, taking disproportionately harsh action could be counterproductive and degenerate into witch-hunting."

A Question of Balance

Incitement to violence is already illegal in most countries, so the very real question is why extra legislation is needed to specifically ban hate speech. Added to this is the question of definition, especially in religious matters, because what may be offensive to some is not to others. This leads governments and judiciaries onto the dangerous ground of determining whose religion is "right."

Added to this is the issue of the correct response to "offense." Is it legitimate to riot and kill innocent people because one's religious feelings have been outraged? The threat of violence in response to religious challenge is just as much a violation of human rights as is any presumed hate speech.

The implementation of hate speech legislation, particularly in the religious sphere, has resulted in serious issues of free speech restriction and violation of religious rights. Perversely, those targeted by such laws often use these same laws to silence dissent, while in other cases the very minorities who are being "protected" end up on the wrong side of the law.

One person's gibe is another's offense, and there's the rub. Definitions and connotations are hard to pin down. What is said is different than what is heard. Communication is not exact. In a democratic society, issues of rights are always a question of balance. Criminalizing religious speech that some may find offensive (and who determines this?) will chill debate and prevent objective analysis. Antidefamation proposals are intended to remove religious debate from the public arena. Any comment that may seem in any way adverse could result in charges of hate speech. Is that what we really want to happen, however much we are persuaded of the importance of protecting others from hate speech?

The old proverb that "sticks and stones may break my bones, but words will never hurt me" may not say it all, but surely it is agreed that it is the actions of hate that maim and kill. Words play a role in the incitement to such violence, and any such incitement is already deemed illegal.

George Orwell in *1984* pointed out the dangers of thought-crime legislation. Policing ideas and speech is surely a highly dangerous practice. The result is a totalitarian society where even thinking wrong is a crime. In order to achieve harmonious thinking, freedom of thought and conscience is condemned. Is that our preferred future? "If liberty means anything at all, it means the right to tell people what they do not want to hear," Orwell concluded. Ultimately, hate speech laws do indeed express "the sad futility of making the unacceptable illegal."

| "It comes as no surprise that the Internet is being used to recruit, disseminate, and incite hatred."

Hate Speech on the Internet Should Be Regulated

Ronald Eissens

Ronald Eissens is the secretariat for the International Network Against Cyber Hate (INACH), an organization based in Amsterdam, the Netherlands. In the following viewpoint, Eissens declares that online hate speech should be regulated to deter extremist groups from using it as a tool to incite racist, religious, or discriminatory violence and crime in real life. He claims that hate groups use the Internet to spread their hateful messages and to threaten and target individuals and organizations through hit lists. Also, Eissens states that regulating online hate speech does not aim to change the bigoted or extremist ideologies of individuals or restrict the freedom of expression, but to deter hate crimes.

As you read, consider the following questions:

1. In the author's view, what causes people to abandon citizenship?

2. How does Eissens support his position that the prohibition of hate speech is not contradictory to free speech?

3. According to Eissens, what is the best protection against hate speech?

Racism, anti-Semitism, Islamophobia, discrimination—more than ever since the Second World War, hate and its ideologies are alive and well, giving cause to misery, conflict, murder, genocide and war. Humanity is repeating its historical mistakes, seemingly unable to learn from the past. The political climate in this world is hardening. The contemporary problems are not only racism, anti-Semitism, Islamophobia and other forms of hate, but also the fact that the idea of citizenship is by and large being abandoned in favor of ethnic, religious and political agendas, which give cause to more 'us and them' feelings on which extremists and fundamentalists feed. Liberals and moderates on all sides are either not being heard or have to shout so loudly that they are being lumped together with the extremists, extremists who, in order to get more support, use the Internet as their tool of choice.

It comes as no surprise that the Internet is being used to recruit, disseminate and incite hatred. The Internet is the biggest information and communication device in the world and neo-Nazis saw the potential in its very early stages, using bulletin board systems (BBS) already in the pre-World Wide Web age. By now, the amount of extremist Web sites runs in the tens of thousands. Hate on the Net has become a virtual nursery for In Real Life crime, the 'Real Life' bit becoming a moot point, since the Internet is an integral part of society, not a separate entity. It is just the latest in communication and dissemination tools which can, as any other tool, be used or abused. Incitement through electronic means is not different from incitement by traditional means. In that sense, you could ask yourself if there is a relation between a paper pamphlet with the text 'kill all Muslims' being handed out in the streets and the actual killing of Muslims. The direct link between those acts will have to be proved while you can say with certainty that calling for the killing of Muslims in a pamphlet (or by other means like the Internet) is incitement and adds to a negative atmosphere towards Muslims, raising the probability of violence. The linkage between racist speech and violations of individual civil liberties is as topical as newspaper headlines. What's more, to some of us it is an everyday reality.

Little Sparks

Little sparks can kindle big fires, which was proved by all the hate speech and dehumanization that was dished-out by media (including the Internet) during the Balkan war, conditioning the public to support any new conflict.

As you will see, the most dominant examples in this booklet of the linkage between incitement on the Internet and actual hate crimes In Real Life are the cases in which Web sites or e-mail were used to deliver the message in the shape of threats, incitement or online hit lists targeting individuals or organizations, sometimes with terrible results.

We all have our separate responsibilities in dealing with incitement to hatred on the Internet, industry, NGOs [nongovernmental organizations] and governments. Which does not mean that we can't cooperate. In fact, it is imperative that we do. Hate has consequences that go further than violence and murder; hate disrupts society in all of its facets, including government and commerce.

In combating hate on the Internet, we do not aim to hinder free speech, nor do we think we will be able to 'change the hearts and minds' of hatemongers. There will always be people who hate. Rather, by using the various national and international anti-hate speech legislation, we aim to curb the communication of hate speech, by this preventing the recruitment of others who do not yet hate, and prevent In Real Life hate crime.

A Whole New Monster

The existence of hate propaganda on the Internet, rather than sapping our will, should mobilize it. Hate speech on the Internet is not just an old threat in new clothes. It is a whole new monster.

The Internet has made hate speech accessible to those who before never would have come into contact with it. It has brought hate speech to children, to the suburbs. One can say generally that those most prone to the messages of hate speech are the marginal and the alienated. It was relatively difficult, prior to the Internet, for hatemongers to seek these people out. The marginal and the alienated, by their very nature, are disconnected socially and politically. There are no organizations for the marginal, clubs for the alienated, connections amongst the disconnected. The Internet allows hatemongers to reach into the privacy and isolation of people's homes, to find the vulnerable, those prone to the message of hate speech, wherever they happen to be.

There are also the sheer numbers. Before the Internet, hate speech was accessible to thousands, those on the mailing lists, those who called in to telephone hate lines, those who could be pamphleteered on the street or in parking lots. Now, through the Internet, hate speech is accessible to millions. The random chance that those susceptible to the siren songs of hatemongers will now hear those songs has increased exponentially because of the Internet.

David Matas, "Countering Hate on the Internet:
Recommendations for Action," 1997. www.media-awareness.ca.

It's a Crime

As for free speech, the European antiracist maxim goes, 'Racism is not an opinion, it's a crime,' or to quote Sartre on anti-Semitism, 'it is not an idea as such, it's a passion.' Having said that, we do recognize and support free speech as an important value in any democratic society. However, we do strongly oppose free speech extremism, the idea that even incitement to murder can be considered free speech, as was the case with the 'Nuremberg Files' [in which an antiabortion activist posted the personal data of abortion clinic workers online to target them for violence], or the abuse of free speech as a means of propagating hate speech and incitement to violence. People tend to think that freedom of speech and the prohibition of hate speech are contradictory. They're not. If we look at the UN International Covenant on Civil and Political Rights, we will see that article 20 quite clearly states that

> any advocacy of national, racial or religious hatred that constitutes *incitement* to discrimination, hostility or violence shall be prohibited by law,

while article 19 states that

> everyone shall have the right to hold opinions without interference. Everyone shall have the right to freedom of expression; this right shall include freedom to seek, receive and impart information and ideas of all kinds, regardless of frontiers, either orally, in writing or in print, in the form of art, or through any other media of his choice. The exercise of the rights provided for in paragraph 2 of this article carries with it special duties and responsibilities. It may therefore be subject to certain restrictions, but these shall only be such as are provided by law and are necessary: (a) For respect of the rights or reputations of others; (b) For the protection of national security or of public order (ordre public), or of public health or morals.

So 143 countries think those are not opposing or conflicting obligations. In fact, most constitutions of Western states show more or less the same situation; an article prohibiting hate speech or discrimination, in close companionship with one securing the freedom of speech. Even the Constitution of the United States (and for that matter, US jurisprudence), much quoted by freedom of speech advocates, does recognize situations in which hate speech can be harmful and should be illegal, for the simple fact that, whereas freedom of speech is a condition for a successful democracy, tolerance is essential for the survival of a democracy. Would one allow hate speech to run rampant, democracy will in the end be destroyed and tyranny would result, bringing with it the abolition of free speech. . . .

[A]t the end of the day, we must conclude that the differences in legislation between the US and Europe are not as big as often perceived. Moreover, neither 'side' will change its constitution, but that is also not necessary. As our work shows, US-European cooperation in fighting hate comes quite easy and is successful. As most Internet providers in the United States have terms of service that strictly prohibit the dissemination of hate speech through their services, it is not as hard as it seems to get material like that removed.

The Best Protection

However, in the end the best protection against hate speech, which can be implemented everywhere no matter what, is education, teaching how information on the Internet can be assessed for its validity and how to recognize the rhetoric of hate. Lots of low-profile Web sites and hate language on Web forums never comes to the attention of law enforcement, or agencies that combat hate on the Net. By and large, it is this material that creates an atmosphere of hate and intolerance, and ultimately generates an environment in which hate becomes acceptable behaviour to people who are infected with prejudiced information. Especially, youth runs the risk of be-

ing misled, indoctrinated and recruited. We think it is imperative to educate and promote attitude change. . . .

Again, the relation between hate speech (online or off-
line) and hate crime is not a question, but an everyday reality.
After all, Auschwitz was not built out of bricks and stones, it
was built with words. Words that were also at the roots of the
Rwandan genocide, the Balkan war and other massacres.

"*Initiatives to combat online hate speech threaten to neuter the Internet's most progressive attribute—the fact that anyone, anywhere, who has a computer and a connection, can express themselves freely on it.*"

Hate Speech on the Internet Should Not Be Regulated

Sandy Starr

In the following viewpoint, Sandy Starr argues that regulating hate speech on the Internet restricts free speech. For example, Starr claims that such initiatives call for online censorship that could be applied to the Bible or Qur'an and artistic and documentary works. The author also maintains that this impedes free and open debate, which is needed to criticize bigoted views and opinions. And he insists that the Internet gives the most radical and fanatical voices false degrees of prevalence and legitimacy. Starr is the science and technology editor for spiked, *a politics and culture online magazine based in London, England.*

Sandy Starr, *The Media Freedom Internet Cookbook*. Vienna, Austria: Organization for Security and Co-operation in Europe (OSCE), 2004. © 2004 Organization for Security and Co-operation in Europe (OSCE). Reproduced by permission.

As you read, consider the following questions:

1. According to Starr, what action does the Internet Watch Foundation advise when encountering racist content online?
2. How does the author support her assertion that hate speech is statistically very uncommon on the World Wide Web?
3. In Starr's view, how could the Remove Jew Watch campaign have more effectively dealt with the Web site Jew Watch?

The Internet continues to be perceived as a place of unregulated and unregulable anarchy. But this impression is becoming less and less accurate, as governments seek to monitor and rein in our online activities.

Initiatives to combat online hate speech threaten to neuter the Internet's most progressive attribute—the fact that anyone, anywhere, who has a computer and a connection, can express themselves freely on it. In the UK, regulator the Internet Watch Foundation (IWF) advises that if you "see racist content on the Internet", then "the IWF and police will work in partnership with the hosting service provider to remove the content as soon as possible".

The presumption here is clearly in favour of censorship—the IWF adds that "if you are unsure as to whether the content is legal or not, be on the safe side and report it". Not only are the authorities increasingly seeking out and censoring Internet content that they disapprove of, but those sensitive souls who are most easily offended are being enlisted in this process, and given a veto over what the rest of us can peruse online.

Take the Additional Protocol to the [international treaty] Convention on Cybercrime, which seeks to prohibit "racist and xenophobic material" on the Internet. The Additional Protocol defines such material as "any written material, any image or any other representation of ideas or theories, which advocates, promotes or incites hatred, discrimination or violence, against any individual or group of individuals, based on race, colour, descent or national or ethnic origin, as well as religion if used as a pretext for any of these factors". It doesn't take much imagination to see how the Bible or the Qur'an could fall afoul of such extensive regulation, not to mention countless other texts and artistic and documentary works.

In accordance with the commonly stated aim of hate speech regulation, to avert the threat of fascism, the Additional Protocol also seeks to outlaw the "denial, gross minimisation, approval or justification of genocide or crimes against humanity". According to the Council of Europe, "the drafters considered it necessary not to limit the scope of this provision only to the crimes committed by the Nazi regime during the Second World War and established as such by the Nuremberg Tribunal, but also to genocides and crimes against humanity established by other international courts set up since 1945 by relevant international legal instruments."

Disconcertingly Authoritarian

This is an instance in which the proponents of hate speech regulation, while ostensibly guarding against the spectre of totalitarianism, are behaving in a disconcertingly authoritarian manner themselves. Aside from the fact that Holocaust revisionism can and should be contested with actual arguments, rather than being censored, the scale and causes of later atrocities such as those in Rwanda or former Yugoslavia are still matters for legitimate debate—as is whether the term "genocide" should be applied to them. The European authorities claim to oppose historical revisionism, and yet they stand to enjoy new powers that will entitle them to impose upon us *their* definitive account of recent history, which we must then accept as true on pain of prosecution.

Remarkably, the restrictions on free speech contained in the Additional Protocol could have been even more severe. Apparently, "the committee drafting the Convention discussed the possibility of including other content-related offences", but "was not in a position to reach consensus on the criminalisation of such conduct". Still, the Additional Protocol as it stands is a significant impediment to free speech, and an impediment to the process of contesting bigoted opinions in free and open debate. As one of the Additional Protocol's more acerbic critics remarks: "Criminalising certain forms of speech is scientifically proven to eliminate the underlying sentiment. Really, I read that on a match cover."

Putting the Internet into Perspective

The Internet lends itself to lazy and hysterical thinking about social problems. Because of the enormous diversity of material available on it, people with a particular axe to grind can simply log on and discover whatever truths about society they wish to. Online, one's perspective on society is distorted. When there are so few obstacles to setting up a Web site, or posting on a message board, all voices appear equal.

The Internet is a distorted reflection of society, where minority and extreme opinion are indistinguishable from the mainstream. Methodological rigour is needed, if any useful insights into society are to be drawn from what one finds online. Such rigour is often lacking in discussions of online hate speech.

For example, the academic Tara McPherson has written about the problem of deep-South redneck Web sites—what she calls "the many outposts of Dixie in cyberspace". As one reads through the examples she provides of neo-Confederate eccentrics, one could be forgiven for believing that "The South Will Rise Again", as the flags and bumper stickers put it. But

Absent Worldwide Conformity

Absent worldwide conformity with the United States' First Amendment as a cornerstone, hate speech will remain available on the Internet despite regulatory efforts of other countries, and its regulation will have implications for the actors on both sides. By the choice of anti-hate state policy, the availability of objectionable content to the users may be limited within a given country, but it will not be blocked out completely due to imperfect filtering technology and numerous technical opportunities of the Internet. By the choice of pro-speech state policy, there is a danger that national ISPs [Internet service providers] and users may face civil and criminal liability once they happen to get into another more restrictive country.

Yulia A. Timofeeva,
"Hate Speech Online: Restricted or Protected?
Comparison of Regulations in the United States and Germany,"
Journal of Transnational Law & Policy, *Spring 2003.*

by that token, the world must also be under dire threat from paedophiles, Satanists, and every other crackpot to whom the Internet provides a free platform.

"How could we narrate other versions of Southern history and place that are not bleached to a blinding whiteness?" asks McPherson, as though digital Dixie were a major social problem. In its present form, the Internet inevitably appears to privilege the expression of marginal views, by making it so easy to express them. But we must remember that the mere fact of an idea being represented online, does not grant that idea any great social consequence.

A Platform for Our Beliefs

Of course, the Internet has made it easier for like-minded individuals on the margins to communicate and collaborate. Mark Potok, editor of the Southern Poverty Law Centre's *Intelligence Report*—which "monitors hate groups and extremist activities"—has a point when he says: "In the 1970s and 80s the average white supremacist was isolated, shaking his fist at the sky in his front room. The net changed that." French minister of foreign affairs Michel Barnier makes a similar point more forcefully, when he says: "The Internet has had a seductive influence on networks of intolerance. It has placed at their disposal its formidable power of amplification, diffusion and connection."

But to perceive this "power of amplification, diffusion and connection" as a momentous problem is to ignore its corollary—the fact that the Internet also enables the rest of us to communicate and collaborate, to more positive ends. The principle of free speech benefits us all, from the mainstream to the margins, and invites us to make the case for what we see as the truth. New technologies that make it easier to communicate benefit us all in the same way, and we should concentrate on exploiting them as a platform for our beliefs, rather than trying to withdraw them as a platform for other people's beliefs.

We should always keep our wits about us, when confronted with supposed evidence that online hate speech is a massive problem. A much-cited survey by the Web and e-mail filtering company SurfControl concludes that there was a 26 percent increase in "Web sites promoting hate against Americans, Muslims, Jews, homosexuals and African Americans, as well as graphic violence" between January and May 2004, "nearly surpassing the growth in all of 2003". But it is far from clear how such precise quantitative statistics can be derived from subjective descriptions of the content of Web sites, and from a subjective emotional category like "hate".

Stirring Up a Panic

SurfControl survey unwittingly illustrates how any old piece of anecdotal evidence can be used to stir up a panic over Internet content, claiming: "Existing sites that were already being monitored by SurfControl have expanded in shocking or curious ways. Some sites carry graphic photos of dead and mutilated human beings." If SurfControl had got in touch with me a few years earlier, I could still easily have found a few photos of dead and mutilated human beings on the Internet for them to be shocked by. Maybe then, they would have tried to start the same panic a few years earlier? Or maybe they wheel out the same shocking claims every year, in order to sell a bit more of their filtering software—who knows?

Certainly, it's possible to put a completely opposite spin on the amount of hate speech that exists on the Internet. For example, Karin Spaink, chair of the privacy and digital rights organization Bits of Freedom, concludes that "slightly over 0.015 percent of all Web pages contain hate speech or something similar"—a far less frightening assessment.

It's also inaccurate to suggest that the kind of Internet content that gets labelled as hate speech goes unchallenged. When it transpired that the anti-Semitic Web site Jew Watch ranked highest in the search engine Google's results for the search term "Jew", a Remove Jew Watch campaign was established, to demand that Google remove the offending Web site from its listings. Fortunately for the principle of free speech, Google did not capitulate to this particular demand—even though in other instances, the search engine has been guilty of purging its results, at the behest of governments and other concerned parties.

Forced to act on its own initiative, Remove Jew Watch successfully used Googlebombing—creating and managing Web links in order to trick Google's search algorithms into associating particular search terms with particular results—to knock Jew Watch off the top spot. This was fair game, and certainly preferable to Google (further) compromising its ranking criteria. Better still would have been either a proper contest of ideas between Jew Watch and Remove Jew Watch, or alternatively a decision that Jew Watch was beneath contempt and should simply be ignored. Not every crank and extremist warrants attention, even if they do occasionally manage to spoof search engine rankings.

Entirely Inadequate

If we ask the authorities to shield us from hate speech today, the danger is that we will be left with no protection from those same authorities tomorrow, once they start telling us what we're allowed to read, watch, listen to, and download.

According to the Additional Protocol to the Convention on Cybercrime, "national and international law need to provide adequate legal responses to propaganda of a racist and xenophobic [fear of foreigners] nature committed through computer systems". But legal responses are entirely *inadequate* for this purpose. If anything, legal responses to hateful opinions inadvertently bolster them, by removing them from the far more effective and democratic mechanism of public scrutiny and political debate.

"Hate speech" is not a useful way of categorizing ideas that we find objectionable. Just about the only thing that the category *does* usefully convey is the attitude of the policy makers, regulators and campaigners who use it. Inasmuch as they can't bear to see a no-holds-barred public discussion about a controversial issue, these are the people who really *hate speech*.

| "If we become accustomed to cumulative acts of burning, trampling and urinating on the flag, all under cover of the Supreme Court, where will that leave the next Martin Luther King?"

Flag Desecration Should Be Restricted

Richard D. Parker

Richard D. Parker is the Paul W. Williams Professor of Criminal Justice at Harvard Law School. According to Parker in the following viewpoint, the arguments against prohibiting flag desecration are flawed. He maintains that such an amendment will not lead to bizarre applications and slippery-slope alterations of the First Amendment, which does not prohibit flag protection. In addition, Parker argues that the American flag does not singularly symbolize one government, one political party, one platform, or one point of view. Therefore, he states that restricting flag desecration does not marginalize—or trample the free speech rights of—citizens with dissenting views.

Richard D. Parker, "Letting the People Decide: The Constitutional Amendment Authorizing Congress to Prohibit Physical Desecration of the Flag of the United States," Testimony Before the Committee on the Judiciary, United States Senate, March 10, 2004, www.legion.org. Reproduced by permission of the author.

As you read, consider the following questions:

1. What arguments support the claim that flag desecration is not a problem, according to the author?
2. How does Parker counter the assertion that prohibiting flag desecration is censorship?
3. In Parker's view, how are supporters of flag protection portrayed?

Whether Congress is empowered, if it chooses, to protect the American flag from physical desecration has been debated for well over a decade. The debate has evolved over time but, by now, a pattern in the argument is clear. Today, I would like to analyze that pattern.

Consistently, the overwhelming majority of Americans have supported flag protection. Consistently, lopsided majorities in Congress have supported it too. In 1989, the House of Representatives voted 371–43 and the Senate 91–9 in favor of legislation to protect the flag. Since that route was definitively blocked by a narrow vote on the Supreme Court in 1990, over two-thirds of the House and nearly two-thirds of the Senate have supported a constitutional amendment to correct the Court's mistake and, so, permit the majority to rule on this specific question. Up to 80% of the American people have consistently supported the amendment.

In a democracy, the burden should normally be on those who would block majority rule—in this case, a minority of the Congress, influential interest groups and most of the media, along with the five Justices who outvoted the other four—to justify their opposition. They have not been reluctant to do so. Indeed, they have been stunningly aggressive. No less stunning has been their unresponsiveness to (and even their seeming disinterest in) the arguments of the popular and congressional majority. What I am going to do is focus on the pattern of their self-justification.

I am going to speak frankly, not just as a law professor, but as an active Democrat. For a disproportionate share of the congressional, interest group and media opposition has been aligned with the Democratic Party. What has pained me, in the course of my involvement with this issue, are attitudes toward our democracy revealed in the structure of the argument against the flag amendment by so many of my fellow Democrats—attitudes that would have seemed odd years ago, when I worked for Senator Robert Kennedy, but that now seem to be taken for granted.

Arguments About (Supposed) Effects of the Constitutional Amendment: Trivialization and Exaggeration

The central focus of argument against the flag amendment involves the (supposedly) likely effects of its ratification. Typically, these effects are—at one and the same time—trivialized and exaggerated. Two general features of the argument stand out: its peculiar obtuseness and the puzzling disdain it exudes for the Congress and for the millions of proponents of the amendment.

A. Trivialization (1) The "What, Me Worry?" Argument. The first trivialization of the amendment's effects is the repeated claim that there is simply no problem for it to address. There are, it is said, few incidents of flag desecration nowadays; and those few involve marginal malcontents who may simply be ignored. The American people's love of the flag, the argument continues, cannot be disturbed by such events. It concludes that, in any event, the flag is "just a symbol" and that the amendment's proponents had better apply their energy to—and stop diverting the attention of Congress from—other, "really important" matters.

What is striking about this argument is not just its condescension to the amendment's supporters and to the Congress which, it implies, cannot walk and chew gum at the same time. Even more striking is its smug refusal to recognize the point of the amendment. The point is not how often the flag has been burned or urinated on or who has been burning it and urinating on it. Rather, the point has to do with our response—especially our official response—to those events. In this case, the key response has been that of the Court and, since 1990, of the Congress. When we are told, officially, that the flag represents just "one point of view" on a par, and in competition, with that of flag desecrators and that flag desecration should not just be tolerated, but protected and even celebrated as free speech; when we get more and more used to acts of desecration; then, "love" of the flag, our unique symbol of national community, is bound gradually to wither—along with other norms of community and responsibility whose withering in recent decades is well known.

To describe what is at stake as "just a symbol" is thus obtuse. The Court's 5–4 decision was not "just a symbol." It was an action of a powerful arm of government, and it had concrete effects. To be sure, its broader significance involved values that are themselves invisible. The issue it purported to resolve is, at bottom, an issue of principle. But would any of us talk of it as "just an issue of principle" and so trivialize it? Surely, the vast majority of members of Congress would hesitate to talk that way. They, after all, voted for a statute to protect the flag. Hence, I would have hoped that the "What, Me Worry?" argument is not one we would hear from them.

(2) The "Wacky Hypotheticals" Argument. The second familiar way of trivializing the amendment's effects is to imagine all sorts of bizarre applications of a law that (supposedly) might be enacted under the amendment. This line of argument purports to play with the terms "flag" and "physically desecrate." Often, the imagined application involves damage to an image (a photo or a depiction) of a flag, especially on clothing—frequently, on a bikini or on underwear. And, often, it involves disrespectful words or gestures directed at an actual

flag or the display of flags in certain commercial settings—a favorite hypothetical setting is a used car lot. This line of argument is regularly offered with a snicker and sometimes gets a laugh.

Its obtuseness should be clear. The proposed amendment refers to a "flag" not an "image of a flag." And words or gestures or the flying of a flag can hardly amount to "physical desecration." In the Flag Protection Act of 1989, Congress explicitly defined a "flag" as taking a form "that is commonly displayed." And it applied only to one who "knowingly mutilates, defaces, physically defiles, burns, maintains on the ground, or tramples" a flag. Why would anyone presume that, under the proposed constitutional amendment, Congress would be less careful and specific?

That question uncovers the attitude beneath the "Wacky Hypotheticals" argument. For the mocking spirit of the argument suggests disdain not only for people who advocate protection of the American flag. It also depends on an assumption that Congress itself is as wacky—as frivolous and as mean-spirited—as many of the hypotheticals themselves. What's more, it depends on an assumption that, in America, law enforcement officials, courts and juries are no less wacky. If the Constitution as a whole had been inspired by so extreme a disdain for our institutions and our people, could its provisions granting powers to government have been written, much less ratified?

Exaggerating the Effects of the Proposed Amendment

B. Exaggeration (1) The "Save the Constitution" Argument. Having trivialized the effects of the proposed amendment, its opponents turn to exaggerating those effects. First, they exaggerate the (supposed) effects of "amending the First Amendment." This might, they insist, lead to more amendments that, eventually, might unravel the Bill of Rights and constitutional government altogether. The argument concludes with a ringing insistence that the people and their elected representatives must not "tinker" or "tamper" or "fool around" with the Constitution.

The claim that the debate is about "amending the First Amendment" sows deep confusion. The truth is that the proposed amendment would not alter "the First Amendment" in the slightest. The First Amendment does not itself forbid protection of the flag. Indeed, for almost two centuries, it was understood to permit flag protection. A 5–4 majority of the Court altered this interpretation, only fifteen years ago. That very narrow decision is all that would be altered by the proposed amendment. The debate thus is about a measure that would restore to the First Amendment its long-standing meaning, preserving the Amendment from recent "tampering."

Adding to the confusion is the bizarre claim that one amendment, restoring the historical understanding of freedom of speech, will somehow lead down a slippery slope to a slew of others undermining the Bill of Rights or the whole Constitution. A restorative amendment is not, after all, the same thing as an undermining amendment. What's more, the process of amendment is no downhill slide. More than 11,000 amendments have been proposed. Only 27—including the Bill of Rights—have been ratified. If there is a "slope," it plainly runs uphill. The scare rhetoric, then, isn't only obtuse. It also manifests disdain for the Congress to which it is addressed.

The greatest disdain manifested by this line of argument, however, is for the Constitution and for constitutional democracy—which it purports to defend. Article V of the Constitution specifically provides for amendment. The use of the amendment process to correct mistaken Court decisions—as it has been used several times before—is vital to maintaining the democratic legitimacy of the Constitution and of judicial review itself. To describe the flag amendment as "tinkering with the Bill of Rights"—when all it does, in fact, is correct a historically aberrant 5–4 decision that turned on the vote of one person appointed to office for life—is to exalt a small, unelected, tenured elite at the expense of the principle and practice of constitutional democracy.

(2) The "Censorship" Argument. The second exaggeration of (supposed) effects of the proposed amendment portrays it as inviting censorship. If Congress prohibits individuals from trashing the American flag, opponents say, it will stifle the freedom of speech. In particular, they continue, it will suffocate expression of "unpopular" or "minority" points of view. It will thereby discriminate, they conclude, in favor of a competing point of view. This line of argument is, essentially, the one adopted by a 5–4 majority of the Court.

It is, however, mistaken. The argument ignores, first of all, the limited scope of laws that the amendment would authorize. Such laws would block no message. They would leave untouched a vast variety of opportunities for self-expression. Indeed, they would even allow expression of contempt for the flag by words—and by deeds short of the "physical" desecration of a flag. Obviously, there must be some limit on permissible conduct. This is so even when the conduct is, in some way, expressive. What's important is this: Plenty of leeway would remain, beyond that narrow limit, for the enjoyment of robust freedom of speech by all.

Secondly, the argument that such laws would impose a limit that discriminates among "competing points of view" misrepresents the nature of the American flag. Our flag does not stand for one "point of view." Ours is not like the flag of Nazi Germany or the Soviet Union—although opponents of the proposed amendment typically make just that comparison. The American flag doesn't stand for one government or one party or one party platform. Instead, it stands for an aspiration to national community despite—and transcending—our differences and our diversity. It doesn't "compete against" contending viewpoints. Rather, it overarches and sponsors their contention. The 5–4 majority on the Court misunderstood the unique nature of our flag. A purpose of the flag amendment is to affirm this uniqueness and, so, correct that mistake.

Thirdly—and most importantly—opponents obtusely ignore the fact that a primary effect of the amendment would be precisely the opposite of the one "predicted" by their scare rhetoric. Far from "censoring" unpopular and minority viewpoints, the amendment would tend to enhance opportunity for effective expression of those viewpoints. A robust system of free speech depends, after all, on maintaining a sense of community. It depends on some agreement that, despite our differences, we are "one," that the problem of any American is "our" problem. Without this much community, why listen to anyone else? Why not just see who can yell loudest? Or push hardest? It is thus for minority and unpopular viewpoints that the aspiration to—and respect for the unique symbol of—national community is thus most important. It helps them get a hearing. The civil rights movement understood this. That is why it displayed the American flag so prominently and so proudly in its great marches of the 1960s.

If we become accustomed to cumulative acts of burning, trampling and urinating on the flag, all under cover of the Supreme Court, where will that leave the next Martin Luther King? Indeed, where will it leave the system of free speech as a whole? As the word goes forth that nothing is sacred, that the aspiration to community is just a "point of view" competing with others, and that any hope of being noticed (if not of getting a hearing) depends on behaving more and more outrageously, won't we tend to trash not just the flag, but the freedom of speech itself? Opponents of the proposed amendment imagine themselves as champions of a theory of free speech—but their argument is based in a strange disdain for it in practice.

Diminished and Dulled

That flag is about values. It's about tradition. It's about America and the men and women who paid an awful price for what we have today.

We honor and cherish members of the Armed Forces and veterans of military service when we honor and protect the flag. Draping the flag over the coffin of a fallen soldier, placing a flag near a grave, or hanging a flag on your house on Memorial Day are all ways we honor and express our appreciation for those who have fought and died defending America. When our laws sanction the physical desecration of the flag, the honor is diminished and the recognition is dulled.

*John Andretti, "Letting the People Decide:
The Constitutional Amendment Authorizing Congress
to Prohibit Physical Desecration of the Flag of the United States,"
Statement by John Andretti, NASCAR Nextel Cup Series Driver,
Testimony Before the Committee on the Judiciary,
United States Senate, March 10, 2004.*

I am, no doubt, preaching to the choir. The Senate voted 91–9 for a flag protection law. Most Senators, therefore, rejected the "censorship" argument in 1989. Now—with the Court absolutely barring such a law on the mistaken ground that any specific protection of the flag discriminates among competing "points of view"—Senators who support protection of the American flag simply have no alternative but to support the proposed constitutional amendment.

Argument About (Supposed) Sources of Support for the Amendment

Most opponents of the amendment don't confine themselves to misrepresenting its effects. Repeatedly, they supplement those arguments with ad hominem, disparaging claims about its supporters as well. Again, they combine strategies of trivialization and exaggeration. What's remarkable is that they seem to assume their generalizations will go unchallenged. They seem to take for granted a denigrating portrayal of others—as well as their own entitlement to denigrate.

The denigration is not exactly overt. It often takes the form of descriptive nouns and verbs, adjectives and adverbs, woven into apparently reasonable sentences. By now, we're so used to these terms of derision that we may not notice them or, worse, take them as signs of "wisdom."

The trivializing portrayal of supporters tends to include references to the (supposedly) "simple" or "emotional" nature of their views—which, in turn, are trivialized as mere "feelings." It's often asserted that they are behaving "frivolously." (Only the opponents, according to themselves, are "thoughtful" people.) Elected officials who back the amendment are said to be "pandering" or "cynical" or taking the "easy" course. (Only opponents, according to themselves, are "courageous" or "honest.") The patriotism of supporters is dismissed as "flag-waving."

The (negatively) exaggerated portrayal tends to include references to the (supposedly) "heated" or "aggressive" or "intolerant" nature of support for the amendment. (Only the opponents, according to themselves, are "deliberative," "restrained" and "respectful of others.") The goal, of course, is to suggest (not so subtly) that the supporters are fanatics or bullies—that they are like a mob that must be stopped before they overwhelm law, order and reason.

A familiar argument fusing trivialization and exaggeration—a *Washington Post* editorial of April 24, 1998 is typical—lumps the flag amendment's supporters with supporters of a great variety of other recently proposed amendments. It smears the former by equating them to others who advocate very different measures more readily belittled as silly or feared as dangerous. There is a name for this sort of argument. It is guilt-by-association. (But then the opponents of the flag amendment, according to themselves, would never employ such rhetoric, would they?)

This is odd. These "thoughtful" people seem to be in the habit of making descriptive generalizations that are not just obtuse but false—not just disdainful but insulting. Why?

Ignoring Counterargument

Part of the answer, I believe, is that opponents of the flag amendment are in another habit. It is the habit of not really listening to the other views. Not listening makes it easier to caricature those views. And, in turn, the caricature of those views makes it easier not to listen to them.

Anyone who's been involved with this issue—on either side—over the years, and who's had an opportunity to see every reference to it in the media across the country, can describe one repeating pattern. Most of the time, the issue is not mentioned. Then, in the weeks before one or another congressional consideration of it, there comes a cascade of editorials and commentary—about 90% hostile to and professing alarm about the amendment. Supporters can describe the other aspect of the pattern: most of the media simply will not disseminate disagreement with that point of view. Speaking from my experience, I can tell you that only a few newspapers have been willing to publish brief responses to what they assume is the one "enlightened" view—their own.

There is an irony here. Those most alarmed about (supposed) discrimination against the views of people who burn or urinate on the American flag are themselves in the habit of discriminating against the views of others who favor protecting the flag. Warning of a (supposed) dampening of robust debate, they dampen robust debate—and they do it in good conscience and with no conscious intent to apply a double standard. What explains such puzzling behavior?

The Value of Public Patriotism

I've characterized the question presented by the flag amendment as involving the value of "community" at the national level. But most opponents seem disinclined to accept that formulation. The question for them seems to involve something they imagine to be narrower than community. For them, the question seems to involve the value of "patriotism." Beneath much of the opposition is, I think, an uneasiness about patriotism as a public value.

I know: Every opponent of the flag amendment insists that he or she is a patriot, that he or she "loves the flag" and, personally, would defend one with life and limb. I don't doubt their sincerity. But I trust I'll be forgiven if I also try to understand the actual behavior of opponents and the language they use to describe the amendment and its source of support. I trust I'll be forgiven if I try to understand all this in terms of a distinction that I think they make between "personal" and "public" patriotism.

I believe that many opponents of the amendment have come to see patriotism as a strictly personal matter—much like religious faith. As such, they affirm its value. But they are, I believe, uneasy about public patriotism. If the uneasiness were focused only on government coercion of patriotism (a coerced flag salute, for example) few would differ. But it is focused, also, on its protection by government (that's what the flag amendment is about), and to some degree it may extend to governmental subsidization and facilitation of public patriotism as well.

For the implicit comparison made by opponents of the flag amendment between patriotism and religious faith carries consequences with it. Two main assumptions lead them to oppose even minor sorts of government assistance to religion. First, there is the assumption that religion is not just deeply personal, but deeply emotional and potentially explosive as well, and that any entanglement of government with religion may therefore produce dangerous conflict and official oppression of freedom and diversity. Second, there is the assumption that, in an increasingly secular age, religious faith is not really terribly relevant to good "governance" anyway—that is, unless "religion" is defined to encompass a wide range of currently accepted secular values.

The same kinds of assumptions underlie both the "exaggeration" and the "trivialization" arguments made by opponents of the flag amendment. First, they imagine that public patriotism taps into raw emotions that threaten to cause conflict and official oppression. Thus they insist that the proposed amendment endangers constitutionalism and freedom. Second, they imagine public patriotism as narrowly militaristic and old-fashioned. In an age of "multiculturalism," on one hand, and of "globalism," on the other, what need is there for it in government and in public life? When the amendment's opponents do affirm the public value of the flag, moreover, they tend to do so by defining "the flag" to stand simply for "the freedom to burn it."

These assumptions and these arguments are perverse. So, too, is the underlying equation of patriotism to religion. For public patriotism is surely basic to motivating broad participation in, and commitment to, our democracy. Far from endangering freedom and political order, it is essential to the effective enjoyment of freedom and maintenance of the legitimacy of government. If national projects, civilian or military, are to be undertaken—if our inherited ideals of liberty and equality are to be realized through concentrated national effort—public patriotism simply has to be valued; its unique symbol should, therefore, be protected.

Let me speak, finally, as a Democrat: When I was growing up, Democrats knew all this. My own hero, Senator Robert Kennedy, would never have doubted the value of public patriotism. He would never have dismissed it as trivial, dangerous or "right wing." I believe that he would have voted—as his son did in 1995 and 1997—to restore to the First Amendment the meaning it had, in effect, for two centuries of our history. That belief encourages me to see this as a truly nonpartisan effort, deserving fully bipartisan support. And, so, it encourages me to urge the United States Senate to permit consideration of the proposed amendment by representatives of the people in the states, submitting this matter to the great democratic process established by Article V of the Constitution.

"It's a fundamentally secular object that represents a fundamentally secular state, but people still call flag-burning desecration."

Flag Desecration Should Not Be Restricted

Robyn Coffey

Robyn Coffey asserts in the following viewpoint that using the flag as a symbol of dissent contributes to social progress and prohibiting these artistic and political expressions infringes on free speech. Coffey maintains that while the flag may symbolize freedom and American principles, demonstrators and artists who burn, destroy, or treat it in other controversial ways do so to express their complex relationships with the United States and to protest the injustices the country has perpetuated. Therefore, the author concludes that the movement against flag desecration essentially aims to silence these dissenting voices. Coffey is a graduate of the School of the Art Institute of Chicago and was a contributor to F Newsmagazine, *the school's student publication.*

As you read, consider the following questions:

1. In Coffey's view, what values have become associated with the flag?

Robyn Coffey, "Desecrating the Flag: The Flag Amendment, Free Speech and Provocation Using Stars and Bars," *F Newsmagazine*, March 2006. Reproduced by permission.

2. How does Coffey counter the surveys that claim the majority of Americans are against flag desecration?

3. According to the author, what is Wafaa Bilal's view of the American flag as an Iraqi?

Throughout the history of cultural controversy, artists have taken it upon themselves to stretch the limits of acceptable expression. Ranging from Artemisia Gentileschi to Théodore Géricault to Hans Haacke, their work has sparked fierce debate and often inspired positive change by exposing offenses against human rights. In contemporary America, citizens frequently use the nation's flag as a symbol in political dissent. But now, Congress is attempting to pass legislation that would threaten their right to freedom of speech.

Under current law, burning, stepping on, drawing on, or representing the flag in artwork in an unflattering manner, are considered acts of political expression which are federally protected by the First Amendment, according to the 1989 Supreme Court ruling *Texas v. Johnson.* That ruling remains an extremely important case for the right to freedom of speech in this nation. But our government administration is attempting (for the fifth time since 1995) to amend the Constitution of the United States to limit that right.

Freedom of Speech: A Right or a Privilege?

The Flag Protection Amendment (Senate Joint Resolution 12) proposes an addition to the Constitution that would grant Congress the power to prohibit physical desecration of the flag of the United States of America. This is basically refined wording to outlaw expressive behaviors such as burning a draft card or a president in effigy, as opposed to garden-variety trash-talking. Apparently, the wording of the First Amendment isn't clear enough: "Congress shall make no law ... abridging the freedom of speech."

The most recent proposition passed the Republican-controlled House as usual last June [2005], and the

Republican-controlled Senate has until the end of this year to make its decision. Senator Orrin Hatch (R-Utah), who is co-sponsoring the bill, told *USA Today* just before the proposal passed the House, "It's important that we venerate the national symbol of our country. Burning, urinating, defecating on the flag this is not speech. This is offensive conduct."

Supreme Court Justice John Paul Stevens described in 1989 the importance of the need to protect that national symbol. "It is more than a proud symbol of the courage, the determination, and the gifts of nature that transformed 13 fledgling Colonies into a world power," he wrote. "It is a symbol of freedom, of equal opportunity, of religious tolerance, and of good will."

It may be only a few red and white lines and a bunch of little stars, but it represents the whole battle our young, headstrong nation fought to get to the top. It's an enduring symbol of "our shared values, of our allegiance to justice, and of those who have sacrificed to defend those principles," according to the Web site of the amendment's other sponsor, Dianne Feinstein (D-California). (Neither Feinstein nor Hatch responded to requests for an interview.)

A resolution proposed by the Veterans of Foreign Wars (VFW) in 2005 points out, "The flag of our nation is being desecrated in every form and the laws of the land are not protecting it."

"The bottom line on the flag amendment," says Joe Davis, director of VFW's public affairs department, "is that one million American service members have died fighting for the ideals and freedoms that the U.S. flag represents. If it's a symbol that's worth saving, it's a symbol that's worth protecting."

The Citizens Flag Alliance [CFA], which supports the amendment, used religious-based research firm Wirthlin Worldwide to conduct a national telephone poll of 8,500 people. The poll, cited on many pro-amendment Web sites, showed that 73 percent of voters believe that a constitutional amendment to protect the flag from desecration would not infringe on their rights to freedom of speech, and 81 percent would vote for it. The survey showed that only 15 percent of voters felt that flag-burning was an appropriate expression of that right. (It also showed that a mere 13 percent of those polled graduated from college, and 78 percent of those polled were white).

However, a similar telephone survey of 1,003 people, conducted by the New England Survey Research Associates in May 2005 for the First Amendment Center, showed that 63 percent of the public is against the amendment, a percentage that has been rising since the annual survey began in 1997.

Senator Hillary Clinton (D-New York) attempted to find a happy medium between laws banning desecration and an actual constitutional amendment, but she was fiercely criticized for her wishy-washy stand. Critics say Clinton is pandering to public opinion for the sake of her bid for President. She told the *New Republic* in July of [2005], "I support federal legislation that would outlaw flag desecration, much like laws that currently prohibit the burning of crosses, but I don't believe a constitutional amendment is the answer. Those few who would destroy a flag are not worthy of the response of amending our founding document."

Many politicians and citizens believe an amendment is the only sure-fire way to protect the American national symbol. The CFA's Web site explains, "The flag remains a single unifying embodiment of our unceasing struggle for liberty, equality, and a basic commitment to others for all citizens, regardless of language, culture and heritage. To protect the laws and freedoms that are based on this unity, we must protect the flag upon which this unity is grounded."

As Justice Stevens wrote in *Texas v. Johnson*, "Sanctioning the public desecration of the flag will tarnish its value both for those who cherish the ideas for which it waves and for those who desire to don the roles of martyrdom by burning it. . . . If ideas [of liberty and equality] are worth fighting for—and history demonstrates that they are—it cannot be true that the flag that uniquely symbolizes their power is not itself worthy of protection from unnecessary desecration."

"If we allow its defacement, we allow our country's gradual decline," added Representative Steve Chabot (R-Ohio) on CBS in June 2003.

Patriotism or Idolatry?

The first nationwide statute prohibiting flag desecration was a Federal Flag Protection Act passed in 1968 to crack down on a rash of burnings in response to the Vietnam War. Millions of demonstrators across the country set fire to American flags to protest the three million victims of the war, racism and sexism, and the fact the government's behavior was simply not supported by its citizens. But it wasn't until the Act of 1968 was overturned in the landmark *Texas v. Johnson* case in 1989 that the Court directly addressed the constitutionality of flag desecration.

In 1984, 27-year-old Gregory Joey Johnson traveled from Georgia to Texas, to protest President Reagan's foreign policy at the Republican National Convention in Dallas. "They had these flags all over the place like a Nuremburg rally," he recently told *F Newsmagazine*. Johnson and several others set fire to a kerosene-soaked flag on the steps of the Capitol Building while demonstrators cheered. (Incidentally, Mayor Daley's office recently declined an offer for Chicago to submit a bid to host the 2008 Republican Convention.)

Johnson describes how he spent a night in a Texas jail cell with physically abusive White Supremacists, and after his bond was posted by locals, eventually returned to Dallas for trial, the only one arrested at the convention to do so. He was convicted by the state of desecration of a venerated object and sentenced to a year in jail and a $2,000 fine.

"[The flag] is a symbol of oppression, international plunder, and murder, the whole global system of exploitation, sweatshopping the planet, and wars of aggression," he says. "The amendment is the government attempting to suppress anti-patriotic activities. There's no disputing people will be political prisoners for burning the flag. [It's] not a criminal [act]. If they're saying they have the right to suppress you because burning the flag harms national unity, well, speaking out against the president harms national unity, too."

He set fire to the flag because "it was a way to really puncture that intense, chauvinistic American atmosphere." He cites the death sentence passed down to award-winning author Salman Rushdie by Iraq's Ayatollah Khomeini, due to alleged blasphemy against Islam in Rushdie's 1989 book *The Satanic Verses*. Only Johnson was blaspheming against the flag.

It's odd how often the flag becomes associated with Christian values (and, for that matter, Nazism). It's a fundamentally secular object that represents a fundamentally secular state, but people still call flag-burning desecration, a word meaning an attack on something sacred, like spray-painting obscenities across a church, or creating insulting images of the Prophet Mohammed. Our government has consistently called upon religious institutions for moral authority, in issues from abolition to gay marriage. The Flag Protection Amendment appeals to those who believe the flag represents freedom and democracy, as well as the three-quarters of the American population who identify themselves as Christian, who are, as Johnson puts it, "indoctrinated from kindergarten to boot camp."

Then we have a Commander-in-Chief who gets a Protestant Evangelist minister to dedicate his presidential inauguration to Jesus. (Bush reportedly told Palestinian Prime Minister Mahmoud Abbas in June 2003, "God told me to strike at al Qaeda and I struck them, and then he instructed me to strike at Saddam, which I did, and now I am determined to solve the problem in the Middle East." Apparently God didn't tell

George W. how.) Bush received flak for signing his autograph on flags at a Republican rally in Michigan in 2003, according to the *Washington Post*, an act that most definitely counts as "physical desecration."

Johnson appealed the conviction, and the case eventually worked its way up to the highest court in the nation. It was the first time the Supreme Court had taken on a flag-burning case addressing First Amendment rights. Included in the testimony presented to the Court were amicus briefs, or "friend-of-the-court" documents designed to bring to light additional information and support not directly related to the case. The briefs were signed by dozens of civil rights organizations and concerned individuals, including artists Jasper Johns, Robert Rauschenburg, Leon Golub, Richard Serra, Faith Ringgold, and Christo. They stated in the document, "Artists do not usually communicate through words, but reach their audiences through the use of symbols and recognized images. Elimination of any particular tool of the trade . . . necessarily limits the visual vocabulary and stifles the creative process."

On June 21, 1989, the Supreme Court ruled 5–4 in Johnson's favor. "If there is a bedrock principle underlying the First Amendment," wrote Justice William Brennan, "it is that the government may not prohibit the expression of an idea simply because society finds the idea itself offensive or disagreeable."

But within four months of the Supreme Court decision, both houses of Congress had reacted by passing a new Flag Protection Act. It states specifically, "Whoever knowingly mutilates, defaces, physically defiles, burns, maintains on the floor or ground, or tramples upon any flag of the United States shall be fined under this title or imprisoned for not more than one year, or both." At midnight on the day it went into effect, people across the country burned flags in protest, and two days later, three people were charged with desecration for setting fire to flags on the steps of the U.S. Capitol.

The Ultimate Futility

The ultimate futility of a flag burning amendment is expressed through the following thought experiment. Suppose I start a company to manufacture objects which resemble the U.S. flag but which bear, on the bottom stripe, the words "This is not a flag." Just to avoid any possible accusation that I am defacing the U.S. flag to create my product, I will print the words "This is not a flag" first, then overlay the stars and stripes. By definition, what I have created cannot be an American flag, because our flag does not contain the words "This is not a flag" on the bottom stripe. Therefore, I would assume that protesters will be able to express themselves freely by burning my product, without violating any law. In fact, they should be able to burn my product with impunity, even partly rolled up with the words "This is not a flag" invisible, as even with those words hidden, the product is not an American flag.

Ethical Spectacle, *"The (Semiotic) Stench of a Burning Flag (Amendment)," February 1996. www.spectacle.org.*

The charges against the three were eventually dropped after a year, following many more demonstrations and legal wrangling, when the Supreme Court again ruled the Flag Protection Act was unconstitutional in *United States v. Eichman.* One of the defendants was a college student named Dread Scott.

Desecration, Also Known as Dissent

Scott had first gained national notoriety in 1988, at age 23, when he created an installation at a gallery operated by the SAIC [School of the Art Institute of Chicago], as part of a group show for minority artists. The installation included a small photomontage on the wall with the headline "What is the proper way to display a US Flag?" It consisted of black and white photographs of South Korean students burning flags and holding "Yankee go home son of bitch" signs, and rows of flag-draped coffins. Below the montage a shelf contained writing implements and a blank book, to encourage audience participation and response, Scott told *F Newsmagazine*. The only problem was, to get to the book, you had to step on Old Glory, laid out in all her splendor right on the floor.

Here's a typical response written in the book, from Scott's Web site (http://dreadscott.home.mindspring.com): "Right now a lady is on the ground crying because of what you have done. I feel you did something wrong and I feel you should be put in jail or have something done to you for this. I love my country and it hurts me to know that you don't. I hope you feel good about yourself for what you are putting people through. You're an asshole."

"The work responded to particular ideas that were part of the discourse of the moment, including Bush running for election on a renewed and reinvigorated patriotism," describes Scott. "My work wasn't an accident. But the fact that it became controversial the way that it did was a bit of an accident," occurring as it did in conjunction with the *Texas v. Johnson* ruling and the contradictory new Flag Protection Act of 1989.

"The right wing was making patriotism compulsory and trying to prescribe only one use for the flag," he explains. "One of the contributions artists make to society is engaging in intellectual inquiry and in critical thought and discourse. There is this illusion of freedom of expression that is promoted in this society. But you cross a line and they will try to suppress you. The forces that were attempting to ban criticism of the flag wanted this work suppressed, and it turned into a bigger fight than they expected."

SAIC Dean Carol Becker wrote in *Art Journal* in 1991, "There was no end to the absurdity and violence mobilized in reaction to this piece. There, at the School of the Art Institute of Chicago, was a symbol of true violence to the American way of life."

President George H.W. Bush publicly denounced it, calling it disgraceful, and Senator Bob Dole issued a statement saying Scott had cast contempt on the flag and invoking the new Flag Protection Act. "The current law covers people who view the display and walk on the flag," wrote Dole, "but not the so-called artist who invited trampling on the flag."

Scott's infamous installation has remained controversial each time he shows it. When it was displayed in New York City, the director of the gallery received death threats and tires on the block were slashed. When it was shown in 2004 at the Phoenix Art Museum, curator David Rubin was chased indoors by an angry mob.

Faith Ringgold, a well-known New York artist who signed Johnson's amicus brief, is renowned for her paintings and her story quilts, which combine text, paint, and appliquéd fabric to make poignant statements about contemporary race relations. They are part of the permanent collections of the Metropolitan, the Guggenheim, and the Museum of Modern Art. Some of Ringgold's work could technically be described as physical desecration, as she frequently employs images of the flag.

"It would be impossible for me to picture the American flag just as a flag, as if that is the whole story," she told *F Newsmagazine.* "I need to communicate my relationship with this flag based on my experience as a black woman in America." One of Ringgold's most strikingly symbolic works is "Flag for the Moon: Die N-----" (1969). At first glance, the painting appears to be a normal American flag, but upon closer examination, the viewer makes out the word "die" superimposed behind the stars, and realizes the stripes consist of the word "n-----" spelled sideways. The piece is part of her Black Light series, in which she experimented with a darker color palette. The flag in "Flag for the Moon" contains no white at all.

Big Brother Meets the Patriot Act

In the art world, such insubordination is often considered a valid and necessary form of political dissent. Public or legislative opinion is rarely swayed by anything less than scandal. As the Supreme Court wrote in 1989, "The First Amendment may indeed best serve its high purpose when it induces a condition of unrest, creates dissatisfaction with conditions as they are, or even stirs people to anger." "It would be a sad day for the free world, at this time of war in the Middle East, if America should cast a blind eye on freedom of speech," says Ringgold.

Wafaa Bilal, an instructor in the photography department at SAIC, spent two years in a refugee camp in Iraq before escaping to the United States in 1992, and has witnessed first-hand the so-called liberty of that country. "From an Iraqi point of view, the American flag cannot and will not stand for freedom or democracy," he says. "It only stands for imperialism." "When I lived in Iraq," Bilal continues, "I had experienced first-hand the destruction inflicted on the people of that country by the United States. For many years, the U.S. supported the regime of Saddam Hussein during the war with Iran. One million people lost their lives during that war. In 1991, Saddam was invited by the U.S. to invade Kuwait. And we all know the result of that invasion. While Americans are enjoying their freedom under the flag, the rest of the world has to suffer because of their government's foreign policy."

Bilal's 1999 installation at the University of New Mexico was vandalized by a protester who felt offended by the graphic, war-themed, anti-American imagery. The installation included a piece called "Total War," a cross-shaped reliquary with a small wooden dildo figure wrapped in a U.S. flag, against a background of pages from the Bible and photographs of Iraqi war victims. Nearby was "Sorrow of Baghdad," a life-size figure with a boar's head and Western-style business suit sitting on a pile of American currency. Every time the sound of a baby crying issued from an adjacent crib, the figure was programmed to respond with laughter. A vandal entered the gallery-turned-mosque and attempted to yank the little crucified doll from the wall. Bilal declined to press charges, explaining the vandal had exactly proved the point the artist was making.

In April 2005, the Secret Service showed up at Columbia College to investigate Chicago artist Al Brandtner's stamp art piece "Patriot Act," included in an exhibition at the Glass Curtain Gallery called *Axis of Evil: The Secret History of Sin.* Brandtner's piece consisted of a page of mock postage stamps with an American flag background and a picture of George W. Bush with gun pointed at his head. Curator Michael Hernandez de Luna told the Associated Press at the time, "It starts questioning . . . the rights of any artist who creates—any writer, any visual artist, any performance artist. It feels like we're being watched."

The fact of the matter is this: The United States of America was founded on the principle that its citizens are free—free to practice their religions, free to gather with whomever they want, and free to speak their minds. This was established in the very first amendment of the Bill of Rights and led to our reputation as the land of the free and the home of the brave. But it's also true that we've made a lot of mistakes and done some embarrassing and shameful things.

"To some people, it's the flag carried by the cavalry that enacted genocide on Native Americans, that dropped bombs on Hiroshima and Nagasaki, and napalm on Vietnam," says

Scott. "It's the flag worn by cops who shoot people in the back. It's the flag of a country pillaging the world." "It's a fascistic amendment," he continues, "and I think it's a dangerous sign of the times that they keep trying to pass it. We're in a moment similar to when Hitler had been elected Chancellor, but the ovens hadn't been built yet."

Periodical Bibliography

The following articles have been selected to supplement the diverse views presented in this chapter.

Victoria Murphy Bennet   "Anonymity & the 'Net," *Forbes*, October 15, 2007.

Current Events   "Speechless? How Free Speech Applies to Schools," April 16, 2007.

Will Doig   "homo.phobo.sphere *n* An Environment Created by Antigay Postings on Internet Blogs That Spreads Hate, Produces Fear, and Is Still Protected by Free Speech," *Advocate*, February 26, 2008.

Charles Gillis   "Righteous Crusader or Civil Rights Menace?" *Maclean's*, April 21, 2008.

Information Week   "Online Child Pornography Defendant Expected to Cooperate," May 11, 2007.

Rod Liddle   "Laws That Constrain Free Speech Bring Out the Childish Bigot in Me," *Spectator*, October 13, 2007.

Adam Liptak   "Hate Speech or Free Speech? What Much of West Bans Is Protected in U.S.," *International Herald Tribune*, June 11, 2008.

Warren Richey   "Ban Upheld on Offering Child Porn," *Christian Science Monitor*, May 20, 2008.

Glen Stassen   "Scapegoat Alert," *Tikkun*, November–December 2007.

Yasmin Whittaker-Kahn   "Saying the Unsayable," *Index on Censorship*, February 2007.

Bob Unruh   "Dis a 'Gay,' Go to Jail!" *World Net Daily*, February 15, 2007.

OPPOSING VIEWPOINTS® SERIES

CHAPTER 2

Should Church and State Be Separate?

Chapter Preface

On May 15, 2008, the California Supreme Court defeated statutes that would limit marriage between a man and a woman. About a month later, on June 17, same-sex marriages were recognized by the state of California, joining Massachusetts and leading Connecticut. On November 4 of that year, however, California voters passed Proposition 8. Titled on the ballot as "Eliminates Right of Same-Sex Couples to Marry," it overturned the May 2008 ruling of the California Supreme Court. During this period, the University of California, Los Angeles, reports that about 18,000 same-sex couples married.

Three days later, on November 7, 2008, thousands of same-sex marriage activists gathered at the Church of Latter-Day Saints in Westwood, California, to protest the Mormon church. The church's members donated an estimated $20 million of the $35.8 million raised for the "Yes-on-8" campaign. For example, the Pattersons, a middle-class Mormon family from Folsom, California, made headlines in October 2008 when they donated $50,000 of their savings to the cause. Says Pam Patterson of her family's contribution, "Was it an easy decision? No. But it was a clear decision, one that had so much potential to benefit our children and their children." According to a television advertisement promoting Proposition 8, Massachusetts public schools now teach elementary-level students that same-sex marriage is acceptable and prevent parents from withdrawing their children from these classes.

Nonetheless, critics assert that the enactment of Proposition 8 violates the separation of church and state. Joseph L. Conn, director of communications of Americans United for the Separation of Church and State, insists, "In effect, you have several of the large faith groups trying to impose their viewpoint on marriage on the whole state. That's really what's going on with this referendum." In addition, Alger Keough, executive pastor of Azure Hills Seventh-Day Adventist Church in Grand Terrace, California, told a California newspaper he believes same-sex marriage is wrong, but that he has no right to force his beliefs upon others and signed a petition against the proposition.

The separation of church and state is a doctrine based on the First Amendment. To Americans such as Joseph L. Conn and Alger Keough, this doctrine created a wall that is absolute. Yet, to others, the wall is intended to protect spiritual freedom from state interference, not to shut religion out of government. Mathew D. Staver, dean of Liberty University School of Law, asserts that the "wall had less to do with the separation of church and *all* civil government than with the separation of federal and state governments." The authors in the following chapter offer their views on how the nation's Founding Fathers envisioned this wall.

"[The] wall of separation between religion and government should be celebrated; it is a bulwark of liberty."

Church and State Should Be Separate

Americans United for Separation of Church and State

Founded in 1947, Americans United for Separation of Church and State is a coalition of religious, educational, and civic leaders. In the following viewpoint, Americans United insists that the First Amendment's separation of church and state is key to religious liberty. According to the coalition, the religious neutrality of the government respects variations of beliefs and protects families' spiritual choices. Also in their view, founding father Thomas Jefferson's doctrine of church-state separation allows diverse faith groups and denominations to coexist and flourish in the United States without the religious violence and strife found in other countries. Therefore, Americans United asserts that his wall of separation has created harmonious religious pluralism and robust spirituality unique to American society.

Americans United for Separation of Church and State, "America's Legacy of Religious Liberty: Pass It On," November 1, 2004. www.au.org. © Americans United for Separation of Church and State. Reproduced by permission.

As you read, consider the following questions:

1. How does Americans United support its claim that religious belief has declined in countries that have or had government-sponsored churches?
2. How is religion "alive and well" in public schools, in the view of Americans United?
3. According to the coalition, how is the separation of church and state good for taxpayers?

Unlike many countries around the world, the United States mandates full religious freedom in its Constitution. No government official or politician can tell you which faith to follow. That very personal decision is made by each individual. Without this right to worship as we see fit, Americans would not be truly a free people.

The constitutional principle that ensures religious liberty is the separation of church and state. The First Amendment says, "Congress shall make no law respecting an establishment of religion or prohibiting the free exercise thereof. . . ." That means simply that government cannot promote religion or interfere with its practice.

Although we sometimes take this vital right for granted today, visionary thinkers fought long and hard to win this freedom. Early American colonies made some denominations their official state religions, and those who dissented were jailed, exiled or even executed. We've come a long way since then.

After the American Revolution, our Founders created a government where true freedom of conscience was protected. It was Thomas Jefferson, our nation's third president and author of the Declaration of Independence, who said that the American people through the First Amendment have built a "wall of separation between church and state." James Madison, the fourth president and Father of the Constitution and Bill of Rights, joined Jefferson in fighting for religious liberty.

Nevertheless, Jefferson's wall—and the very concept of church-state separation—have become the subject of many misunderstandings over the years. Here are the facts:

Separation of Church and State Is Good for Religion

The United States is one of the most religious nations on earth. The overwhelming majority of Americans say they believe in God, and many attend worship services regularly. In contrast, in some European nations where religion still gets government support, interest in faith is falling, and many people no longer go to services.

Surveys of residents of Europe find declining belief in religion. In England, Germany, Sweden, Denmark and the Netherlands, fewer than 1 in 10 people attend religious services. Fifty-five percent of people in Sweden say God is not important to them. Yet many of these countries have government-established churches or had them until recently.

Compare those figures to the U.S. equivalents: Here, nearly 50 percent attend religious services regularly. Eighty-three percent say they have prayed within the past week; 95 percent believe in God.

It seems that the failure to separate church and state hurts religion. Why is that? Here's the answer: Freedom and competition are good for religion. When houses of worship are dependent on government for support, religion loses its vitality. In America, religious groups rely on voluntary contributions. This policy makes them more robust.

Church-state separation also guarantees the right of religious groups to speak out on issues of justice, ethics and morality. In countries where religion receives tax support, clergy usually are wary of criticizing the government. After all, they don't want to bite the hand that feeds them! Because religious groups in America are truly independent, they feel no such constraints. They are free to try to persuade other Americans toward their perspective.

Madison was well aware of this. In his home state of Virginia, Madison noted that severing the ties between religion and government increased interest in religion and made the citizenry more virtuous. In 1819, he wrote, "The number, the industry, and the morality of the priesthood and the devotion of the people have been manifestly increased by the total separation of the church from the state."

[French political thinker] Alexis de Tocqueville made a similar observation in his well-known book *Democracy in America*. Tocqueville, who traveled extensively in the United States in the early part of the 19th century, noted that religion was much stronger in America than in Europe.

After talking with both ministers and church members of different faiths, Tocqueville reported, "[T]hey all attributed the peaceful dominion of religion in their country mainly to the separation of church and state. I do not hesitate to affirm that during my stay in America I did not meet a single individual, of the clergy or the laity, who was not of the same opinion on this point."

Tocqueville's view is not surprising. By guaranteeing the free exercise of faith and barring the establishment of religion, the First Amendment protects houses of worship from government interference and places a premium on their independence.

In addition, because church-state separation prevents the government from taking sides in religious disputes, it creates a type of "religious free market" whereby various faiths are free to spread their views and win new converts.

Most American religious leaders appreciate the protections guaranteed by our Constitution. They have no desire to see any religion, including their own, favored by the government.

Only a small—but vocal and well-organized—minority questions our heritage of religious liberty and campaigns to see their faith enshrined in law.

Separation of Church and State Is Good for Families

Thanks to the separation of church and state, you are in complete control of the religious upbringing of your children. Government institutions, including the public school system, are not permitted to coerce your children to adopt new and different religions.

Religious traditions differ on matters of doctrine and practice. Even among the different branches of Christianity, there are wide variations of belief. These are not meaningless distinctions. People take them very seriously. Due to the separation of church and state, the government remains neutral on these disputes. This gives you the right to decide which religious views you will adopt and which you will choose for your children.

Protecting youngsters from government coercion is one of the most important things the First Amendment does. In 1962 and '63, the Supreme Court struck down mandatory worship in public schools. The court did not ban voluntary prayer and Bible reading or "kick God out of the schools," as some mistakenly claim. Rather, it ruled that parents—not politicians, bureaucrats or school officials—have the right to make decisions about their children's religious training. Why would we want to have it any other way?

Religion is alive and well in America's public schools. The difference today is that it is *voluntary* religion. Student-run religious clubs meet on high school campuses outside class hours all over the country, but no youngster is compelled or pressured to attend. In fact, *Charisma*, a Christian magazine, reports that 10,000 Bible clubs meet in America's schools. Public schools are not "religion-free" zones.

Reproductive Choice

The Supreme Court's 1973 ruling in *Roe v. Wade* and *Doe v. Bolton* recognized a constitutional right to privacy that covered not only the right to use contraception but also the right of a woman to choose to terminate a problem pregnancy. *Roe* has so far stood the test of time and public opinion, but the Supreme Court has allowed state legislatures to impose some restrictions on the right to choose, such as waiting periods, mandatory presentation of misinformation to women seeking abortions and burdensome or excessive regulation of reproductive health clinics.

Although the Supreme Court has dealt with reproductive choice as a "constitutional right to privacy" matter, the issue also clearly has to do with "establishment" and "free exercise." Government restriction of choice is tantamount to establishing or preferring one religious perspective over all others, that is, the theological notion that "personhood" begins at conception as opposed to the view that "personhood" begins much later, such as after the cerebral cortex is sufficiently developed to permit the possibility of consciousness or at birth. Governmental restriction on choice also runs counter to "free exercise," which is largely synonymous with freedom of conscience.

Edd Doerr,
"Part 1.4: 'The Importance of Church State Separation,"
Toward a New Political Humanism. *Barry F. Seidman*
and Neil J. Murphy, eds. Amherst, NY: Prometheus Books, 2004.

Students may pray or read scripture at any time during the school day that the academic schedule permits, but the decision must be theirs. Schools may not sponsor devotional activities, but they are allowed to offer instruction about religion from an academic perspective. They may teach but not preach or usurp the rightful role of parents. The high court's decisions about our schools have struck the right balance.

Separation of Church and State Is Good for Taxpayers

Many colonial-era Americans were strongly opposed to taxation to support government-favored churches. They vehemently resented being forced to turn over their hard-earned money to support religions whose doctrines they considered wrong or even dangerous.

Separation of church and state ended that unfair arrangement. Once the institutions of religion and government were separated, all houses of worship were set free to raise financial support through private donations, not coercion.

Today, this system means *you* get to decide how much money you contribute to religious groups. Unlike some countries, the United States no longer levies church taxes on anyone or compels financial support for religion. Our religious institutions have thrived under this arrangement, receiving an estimated $81 billion in contributions annually.

Despite the generosity of the American people in supporting religion voluntarily, there have been occasional calls to require the taxpayer to fund religious endeavors. The American people have resisted this. Over the years, several states have held referenda on proposals to fund church-run schools and other religious institutions with public money. All have been voted down, usually by wide margins.

Separation of Church and State Is Good for America

Few countries have as much religious diversity as ours. One scholar of religion has estimated that 2,000 faith groups and denominations are active in America.

All of these traditions exist side by side and get along extraordinarily well. The United States has been spared the worst excesses of inter-religious conflict. The Balkans, Northern Ireland, the Middle East and other regions have been torn apart by religious violence that sometimes has gone on for centuries. Americans have been spared most of this tension, thanks to our wise policy of church-state separation.

Separation of church and state works so well that the principle has been celebrated by scholars and political leaders across the spectrum. Liberals and conservatives, Democrats, Republicans and Independents have hailed this vital concept.

One of the most powerful endorsements came from President John F. Kennedy, who in a 1960 speech remarked, "I believe in an America that is officially neither Catholic, Protestant or Jewish—where no public official either requests or accepts instructions on public policy from the pope, the National Council of Churches or any other ecclesiastical source, where no religious body seeks to impose its will directly or indirectly upon the general populace or the public acts of its officials and where religious liberty is so indivisible that an act against one church is treated as an act against all."

Sen. Barry Goldwater, a noted conservative Republican, also strongly backed church-state separation. In a 1994 essay, Goldwater wrote, "I am a conservative Republican, but I believe in democracy and the separation of church and state. The conservative movement is founded on the simple tenet that people have the right to live life as they please as long as they don't hurt anyone else in the process."

In a famous 1981 speech, Goldwater said, "By maintaining the separation of church and state, the United States has avoided the intolerance which has so divided the rest of the world with religious wars. . . . Can any of us refute the wisdom of Madison and the other framers? Can anyone look at the carnage in Iran, the bloodshed in Northern Ireland or the bombs bursting in Lebanon and yet question the dangers of injecting religious issues into the affairs of state?"

The United States has a well-deserved reputation as a beacon for religious liberty around the world. Throughout our history, immigrants have come to our shores seeking the right to worship as they saw fit. Our nation's policy of separation of church and state has ensured religious freedom and made our country a model for others to follow.

People of goodwill may disagree about some of the more contentious issues surrounding church-state separation. But there should be no argument about the value of the underlying principle. Jefferson's wall of separation between religion and government should be celebrated; it is a bulwark of liberty. Religious freedom is one of America's greatest legacies. We must ensure that our children and grandchildren enjoy it as well.

> *"[T]he phrase 'separation of church and state' and its attendant metaphoric formulation, 'a wall of separation,' have often been expressions of exclusion, intolerance, and bigotry."*

Church and State Should Not Be Separate

Daniel L. Dreisbach

Daniel L. Dreisbach is a professor in the School of Public Affairs at American University in Washington, DC, and author of Thomas Jefferson and the Wall of Separation Between Church and State. *In the following viewpoint, Dreisbach alleges that the doctrine of church-state separation has been misconstrued throughout American history. The author claims that American president Thomas Jefferson, who penned the dividing "wall" metaphor, originally intended that it separate the federal government from state governments and churches, protecting religious freedom. However, Dreisbach suggests that this metaphor has been recast in several landmark cases and appropriated by groups who are intolerant of religious influence and values in public life and politics.*

Daniel L. Dreisbach, "The Mythical 'Wall of Separation': How a Misused Metaphor Changed Church State Law, Policy, and Discourse," *Heritage Foundation*, June 23, 2006. Reproduced by permission.

As you read, consider the following questions:

1. What did Jefferson's Danbury letter endorse, as stated by the author?

2. According to Dreisbach, what role did Justice Hugo L. Black have in redefining the separation between church and state?

3. In the author's view, which groups have relied upon the separation of church and state?

No metaphor in American letters has had a more profound influence on law and policy than Thomas Jefferson's "wall of separation between church and state." Today, this figure of speech is accepted by many Americans as a pithy description of the constitutionally prescribed church–state arrangement, and it has become the sacred icon of a strict separationist dogma that champions a secular polity in which religious influences are systematically and coercively stripped from public life.

In our own time, the judiciary has embraced this figurative phrase as a virtual rule of constitutional law and as the organizing theme of church–state jurisprudence, even though the metaphor is nowhere to be found in the U.S. Constitution. In *Everson v. Board of Education* (1947), the United States Supreme Court was asked to interpret the First Amendment's prohibition on laws "respecting an establishment of religion." "In the words of Jefferson," the justices famously declared, the First Amendment "was intended to erect 'a wall of separation between church and State' . . . [that] must be kept high and impregnable. We could not approve the slightest breach."

In the half-century since this landmark ruling, the "wall of separation" has become the *locus classicus* [classical package] of the notion that the First Amendment separated religion and the civil state, thereby mandating a strictly secular polity. The trope's continuing influence can be seen in Justice John Paul Stevens's recent warning that our democracy is threatened "[w]henever we remove a brick from the wall that was designed to separate religion and government."

What is the source of this figure of speech, and how has this symbol of strict separation between religion and public life come to dominate church–state law and policy? Of Jefferson's many celebrated pronouncements, this is one of his most misunderstood and misused. I would like to challenge the conventional, secular myth that Thomas Jefferson, or the constitutional architects, erected a high wall between religion and the civil government. . . .

Building a "Wall of Separation"

On New Year's Day, 1802, President Jefferson penned a missive to the Baptist Association of Danbury, Connecticut. The Baptists had written the President a "fan" letter in October 1801, congratulating him on his election to the "chief Magistracy in the United States." They celebrated Jefferson's zealous advocacy for religious liberty and chastised those who had criticized him "as an enemy of religion[,] Law & good order because he will not, dares not assume the prerogative of Jehovah and make Laws to govern the Kingdom of Christ."

In a carefully crafted reply, Jefferson endorsed the persecuted Baptists' aspirations for religious liberty:

> Believing with you that religion is a matter which lies solely between Man & his God, that he owes account to none other for his faith or his worship, that the legitimate powers of government reach actions only, & not opinions, I contemplate with sovereign reverence that act of the whole American people which declared that *their* legislature should "make no law respecting an establishment of religion, or prohibiting the free exercise thereof," thus building a wall of separation between Church & State.

Although today Jefferson's Danbury letter is thought of as a principled statement on the prudential and constitutional relationship between church and state, it was in fact a political statement written to reassure pious Baptist constituents that Jefferson was indeed a friend of religion and to strike back at the Federalist—Congregationalist establishment in Connecticut for shamelessly vilifying him as an infidel and atheist in the recent campaign. James H. Hutson of the Library of Congress has concluded that the President "regarded his reply to the Danbury Baptists as a political letter, not as a dispassionate theoretical pronouncement on the relations between government and religion."

Jefferson's Understanding of the "Wall"

Throughout his public career, including two terms as President, Jefferson pursued policies incompatible with the "high and impregnable" wall the modern Supreme Court has erroneously attributed to him. For example, he endorsed the use of federal funds to build churches and to support Christian missionaries working among the Indians. The absurd conclusion that countless courts and commentators would have us reach is that Jefferson routinely pursued policies that violated his own "wall of separation."

Jefferson's wall, as a matter of federalism, was erected between the national and state governments on matters pertaining to religion and not, more generally, between the church and *all* civil government. In other words, Jefferson placed the federal government on one side of his wall and state governments and churches on the other. The wall's primary function was to delineate the constitutional jurisdictions of the national and state governments, respectively, on religious concerns, such as setting aside days in the public calendar for prayer, fasting, and thanksgiving. Evidence for this jurisdictional or structural understanding of the wall can be found in both the texts and the context of the correspondence between Jefferson and the Danbury Baptist Association. . . .

Jefferson's refusal, as President, to set aside days in the public calendar for religious observances contrasted with his actions in Virginia where, in the late 1770s, he framed "A Bill for Appointing Days of Public Fasting and Thanksgiving" and, as governor in 1779, designated a day for "publick and solemn thanksgiving and prayer to Almighty God."

How can Jefferson's public record on religious proclamations in Virginia be reconciled with the stance he took as President of the United States? The answer, I believe, is found in the principle of federalism. Jefferson firmly believed that the First Amendment, with its metaphoric "wall of separation," prohibited religious establishments by the federal government only. Addressing the same topic of religious proclamations, Jefferson elsewhere relied on the Tenth Amendment, arguing that because "no power to prescribe any religious exercise . . . has been delegated to the General [i.e., federal] Government[,] it must then rest with the States, as far as it can be in any human authority." He sounded the same theme in his Second Inaugural Address, delivered in March 1805:

> In matters of religion, I have considered that its free exercise is placed by the constitution independent of the powers of the general [i.e., federal] government. I have therefore undertaken, on no occasion, to prescribe the religious exercises suited to it; but have left them, as the constitution found them, under the direction and discipline of State or Church authorities acknowledged by the several religious societies.

These two statements were, in essence, Jefferson's own commentary on the Danbury letter, insofar as they grappled with identical issues. Thus, as a matter of federalism, he thought it inappropriate for the nation's chief executive to proclaim days for religious observance; however, he acknowledged the authority of state officials to issue religious proclamations. In short, Jefferson's "wall" was erected between the federal and state governments on matters pertaining to religion.

The Wall That Black Built

The phrase "wall of separation" entered the lexicon of American constitutional law in 1879. In *Reynolds v. United States*, the U.S. Supreme Court opined that the Danbury letter "may be accepted almost as an authoritative declaration of the scope and effect of the [first] amendment thus secured." Although the Court reprinted the entire second paragraph of Jefferson's letter containing the metaphorical phrase, Jefferson's language is generally characterized as *obiter dictum* [said in passing].

Nearly seven decades later, in the landmark case of *Everson v. Board of Education* (1947), the Supreme Court rediscovered the metaphor: "In the words of Jefferson, the [First Amendment] clause against establishment of religion by law was intended to erect 'a wall of separation between church and State'. . . . That wall," the justices concluded in a sweeping separationist declaration, "must be kept high and impregnable. We could not approve the slightest breach." Jefferson's words were woven neatly into the *Everson* ruling, which, like *Reynolds*, was replete with references and allusions to history, especially the roles played by Jefferson and [American president] Madison in the Virginia disestablishment struggles.

Justice Hugo L. Black, who authored the Court's ruling, likely encountered the metaphor in briefs filed in *Everson*. In an extended discussion of American history that highlighted Virginia's disestablishment battles and supported the proposition that "separation of church and state is a fundamental American principle," attorneys for the American Civil Liberties Union quoted the single clause in the Danbury letter that contains the "wall of separation" image. The challenged state statute, the ACLU ominously concluded, "constitutes a definite crack in the wall of separation between church and state. Such cracks have a tendency to widen beyond repair unless promptly sealed up."

The trope's current fame and pervasive influence in popular, political, and legal discourse date from its rediscovery by the *Everson* Court. The Danbury letter was also cited frequently and favorably in the cases that followed *Everson.* In *McCollum v. Board of Education* (1948), the following term, and in subsequent cases, the Court essentially constitutionalized the Jeffersonian phrase, subtly and blithely substituting Jefferson's figurative language for the literal text of the First Amendment. In the last half of the 20th century, it became the defining motif for church–state jurisprudence.

The "high and impregnable" wall central to the past 50 years of church–state jurisprudence is not Jefferson's wall; rather, it is the wall that Black—Justice Hugo Black—built in 1947 in *Everson v. Board of Education.* . . .

By extending its prohibitions to state and local jurisdictions, Black turned the First Amendment, as ratified in 1791, on its head. A barrier originally designed, as a matter of federalism, to separate the national and state governments, and thereby to preserve state jurisdiction in matters pertaining to religion, was transformed into an instrument of the federal judiciary to invalidate policies and programs of state and local authorities. As the normative constitutional rule applicable to all relationships between religion and the civil state, the wall that Black built has become the defining structure of a putatively secular polity.

Reconceptualizing the First Amendment

After two centuries, Jefferson's trope is enormously influential, but it remains controversial. The question bitterly debated is whether the wall illuminates or obfuscates the constitutional principles it metaphorically represents.

The wall's defenders argue that it promotes private, voluntary religion and freedom of conscience in a secular polity. The wall prevents religious establishments and avoids sectarian conflict among denominations competing for governmental favor and aid. An impenetrable barrier prohibits not only the formal recognition of, and legal preference for, one par-

The ACLU and the Separation of Church and State

For the past forty years the ACLU [American Civil Liberties Union] has used every legal machination to make the display of Christmas trees illegal if placed in a public institution or on property where there is even the remotest connection to a tax dollar. They've bludgeoned America with their claim that such displays violate the separation of church and state. The display of the Ten Commandments? Illegal, they say. Prayer in school? Prohibited, they charge. The mere mention of God at a graduation ceremony—grounds for a law suit. The display of a Menorah—the next morning the ACLU is at the court steps already litigating.

How strict are they in their interpretation of separation of church and state? In Pittsburgh they went so far as to demand that a municipal parking lot be off limits to those parking there to visit a local Christmas display at a nearby church.

Aryeh Spero, "*The ACLU: Enemy of America and Christianity,*" Human Events, *July 20, 2007. www.humanevents.com.*

ticular church (or denomination), but also all other forms of government assistance or encouragement for religious objectives. A regime of strict separation, defenders insist, is the best, if not the only, way to promote religious liberty, especially the rights of religious minorities.

I contend that the graphic wall metaphor has been a source of much mischief in modern church–state jurisprudence. It has reconceptualized—indeed, I would say, *mis*conceptualized—First Amendment principles in at least two important ways.

First, Jefferson's trope emphasizes *separation* between church and state, unlike the First Amendment, which speaks in terms of the non-establishment and free exercise of religion. (Although these terms are often conflated today, in the lexicon of 1802, the expansive concept of "separation" was distinct from the institutional concept of "non-establishment.") . . .

Second, the very nature of a wall further reconceptualizes First Amendment principles. A wall is a bilateral barrier that inhibits the activities of both the civil state and religion, unlike the First Amendment, which imposes restrictions on civil government only. The First Amendment, with all its guarantees, was entirely a check or restraint on civil government, specifically Congress. The free press guarantee, for example, was not written to protect the civil state from the press; rather, it was designed to protect a free and independent press from control by the federal government.

Similarly, the religion provisions were added to the Constitution to protect religion and religious institutions from corrupting interference by the federal government and not to protect the civil state from the influence of, or overreaching by, religion. The wall, however, is a bilateral barrier that unavoidably restricts religion's ability to influence public life; thus, it necessarily and dangerously exceeds the limitations imposed by the First Amendment.

Let me say as an aside: I do not believe that many so-called strict separationists are, in fact, consistent adherents of their "high and impregnable" wall. Virtually all advocate the separation of religion (and religious influences) from the civil state and public life, but few consistently argue that civil government should be completely separated from the concerns of the church. Few strict separationists are willing, even in strict adherence to a wall-of-separation principle, to exempt churches, clergy, and religious entities from the civil state's generally applicable civil rights, criminal, employment, tax, and zoning laws, as well as health and safety regulations.

Is their wall a single-sided wall that imposes restrictions on the church but not on the civil state? All too often, the wall of separation is used to silence the church and to limit its reach into public life, but it is rarely used to restrain the civil state's meddling in, and restraint of, the church.

Legacy of Intolerance

We must confront the uncomfortable fact that, for much of American history, the phrase "separation of church and state" and its attendant metaphoric formulation, "a wall of separation," have often been expressions of exclusion, intolerance, and bigotry. These phrases have been used to silence people and communities of faith and to exclude them from full participation in public life. . . .

In the bitter presidential campaign of 1800, Jeffersonian Republicans cynically advocated the rhetoric and policy of separation, not to promote religious worship and expression, but to silence the Federalist clergy who had vigorously denounced Jefferson as an infidel and atheist. (Two centuries later, the American Civil Liberties Union and its allies continue to use these phrases to silence people and communities of faith that seek to participate in the public marketplace of ideas armed with ideas informed by spiritual values.)

Not surprisingly, this separationist rhetoric returned to fashion in the 1830s and 1840s and, again, in the last quarter of the 19th century when waves of Catholic immigrants, with their peculiar liturgy and resistance to assimilation into the Protestant establishment, arrived on American shores. Nativist elements, including the Know Nothings and later the Ku Klux Klan, embraced separationist rhetoric and principles in a continuing, and often violent, campaign to restrict the role of Catholics in public life.

Again, in the mid-20th century, the rhetoric of separation was revived and ultimately constitutionalized by anti-Catholic elites, such as Hugo Black, and the American Civil Liberties Union and Protestants and Other Americans United for the Separation of Church and State, who feared the influence and wealth of the Catholic Church and perceived parochial education as a threat to public schools and democratic values. . . .

Why It Matters

Why should we care about this metaphor today? We should care because the wall is all too often used to separate religion from public life, thereby promoting a religion that is essentially private and a state that is strictly secular. This would have alarmed the founders because they viewed religion, to paraphrase George Washington's words, as an indispensable support for social order and political prosperity.

Today, the wall is the cherished emblem of a strict separationist dogma intolerant of religious influences in the public square. Federal and state courts have used the "wall of separation" concept to justify censoring private religious expression (such as Christmas crèches) in public fora; stripping public spaces of religious symbols (such as crosses); denying public benefits (such as education vouchers) for religious entities; and excluding religious citizens and organizations (such as faith-based social welfare agencies) from full participation in civic life on the same terms as their secular counterparts. The systematic and coercive removal of religion from public life not only is at war with our cultural traditions insofar as it evinces a callous indifference toward religion, but also offends basic notions of freedom of religious exercise, expression, and association in a democratic and pluralistic society.

The "high and impregnable" wall constructed by the Supreme Court inhibits religion's ability to inform the public ethic and policy, deprives religious citizens of the civil liberty to participate in politics armed with ideas informed by their spiritual values, and infringes the right of religious communities and institutions to extend their prophetic ministries into the public square. Jefferson's metaphor, sadly, has been used to silence the religious voice in the marketplace of ideas and, in a form of religious apartheid, to segregate faith communities behind a restrictive barrier.

The wall metaphor provides little practical guidance for the application of First Amendment principles to real-world church–state controversies, short of recommending a policy of absolute separation. Few courts or even separationist partisans, however, contend that a total and perfect separation is practical or mandated by the Constitution. In short, the wall is incapable of providing specific, practical guidelines that can be implemented in difficult disputes that require a delicate balancing of competing constitutional values, such as the freedoms of speech, association, religious exercise, and the non-establishment of religion.

The wall is politically divisive. Because it is so concrete and unyielding, its very invocation forecloses meaningful dialogue regarding the prudential and constitutional role of religion, faith communities, and religious citizens in public life. The uncritical use of the metaphor has unnecessarily injected inflexibility into church–state debate, fostered distortions and confusion, and polarized students of church–state relations, inhibiting the search for common ground and compromise on delicate and vexing issues. . . .

The Trouble with Metaphors in the Law

Metaphors enrich language by making it dramatic and colorful, rendering abstract concepts concrete, condensing complex concepts into a few words, and unleashing creative and analogical insights. Who can imagine Abraham Lincoln's articulation of his great cause absent the biblical allusion to a "house divided" or Winston Churchill's Cold War charge without mention of the "iron curtain?" Metaphors, however, must be used with caution in the law, especially in judicial opinions and statutes. Legal discourse, unlike much political rhetoric, requires precision of expression, strict and orderly adherence to rules set forth in legislative enactments or past judicial decisions.

Metaphor is a valuable literary device, but its uncritical use can lead to confusion and distortion. At its heart, metaphor compares two or more things that are not in fact identical; a metaphor's literal meaning is used nonliterally in a comparison with its subject. While the comparison may yield useful insights, the dissimilarities between the metaphor and its subject, if not recognized, can distort or pollute one's understanding of the actual subject.

Metaphors inevitably graft onto their subjects connotations, emotional intensity, and/or cultural associations that transform the understanding of the subject as it was known pre-metaphor. If attributes of the metaphor are erroneously or misleadingly assigned to the subject and the distortion goes unchallenged, the metaphor may reconceptualize or otherwise alter the understanding of the underlying subject. The more appealing and powerful a metaphor, the more it tends to supplant or overshadow the original subject and the more one is unable to contemplate the subject apart from its metaphoric formulation. Thus, distortions perpetuated by the metaphor are sustained and magnified.

Jefferson's phrase powerfully illustrates this. Although the metaphor may felicitously express some aspects of the First Amendment, it seriously misrepresents or obscures others. . . .

| "[We] ought to allow religious organizations to compete for funding on an equal basis, not for the sake of faith, but for the sake of results."

More Faith-Based Charitable Organizations Should Receive Federal Funds

George W. Bush

George W. Bush is the forty-third president of the United States. In the following viewpoint taken from a conference speech, Bush declares that faith-based charitable organizations play an important role in improving America and should be able to compete equally for federal funds. He insists that corporate foundations only allot a small percentage of their grants to faith-based charitable organizations, when such contributions are permitted at all. Consequently, Bush asserts that giving faith-based charitable organizations social service funds with less bureaucracy and restrictions recognizes the objectives they achieve, not their religious beliefs.

As you read, consider the following questions:

1. According to Bush, what "quiet transformation" is taking place in America?

George W. Bush, "President Highlights Faith-Based Results at National Conference," in Whitehouse.gov, March 9, 2006.

2. What is the importance of Bush's "score card"?

3. In the author's view, what specifically in Washington, D.C.'s culture needs to change regarding faith-based programs?

We meet at a time of great hope for the country. In my State of the Union—I stated this, and I believe it firmly—that America is witnessing a quiet transformation, a revolution of conscience, in which a rising generation is finding that a life of personal responsibility is a life of fulfillment. Part of being personally responsible in America is to love a neighbor like you'd like to be loved yourself. And for those of you who are finding those who have heard the call to help interface with those in need, I thank you from the bottom of my heart. You represent the true strength of the United States of America.

Statistics matter, and you'll hear me talk about some of the results of the faith-based initiative. It's hard to be a results-oriented society unless you actually focus on results. I'd like to share some results with you to boost my belief that there is a quiet transformation taking place. Violent crime rates have fallen to their lowest level since the 1970s. Welfare cases have dropped by more than half. Drug use amongst youth is down 19 percent since 2001. There are fewer abortions in America than at any point in the last three decades. The number of children born to teenage mothers has fallen for a dozen years in a row. I attribute the success of these statistics to the fact that there are millions of our fellow citizens all working to help people who hurt, working toward a better tomorrow.

There's a lot of work to be done, obviously. We still have pockets of poverty where people wonder whether or not the American experience belongs to them. We have places where there is hopelessness and despair. We've got people that are homeless. We've got addicts trapped into a, what appears to them, I'm certain, kind of a never-ending cycle of despondency.

Focusing on Results

In answering the challenges, staying focused on helping change America one person at a time is a vital part of government, corporate America, philanthropic America, and the faith and community-based programs. It's got to be our continued focus. Even though statistics are improving, so long as we find anybody who hurts, we all should recognize that we hurt. It's the collective conscience of America that really helps define the nature of our country, and it gives me great optimism for the future of our country. . . .

We've got fantastic corporate foundations in America who recognize that we all ought to focus on results, not process; that the question government and private philanthropy ought to ask is, does the program get the results that we all want, as opposed to, what is the nature of the people trying to get results? When you focus on results, all of a sudden it becomes crystal clear how best to spend resource dollars to achieve certain objectives.

And today, I met with some folks earlier that talked about their foundations and how their foundations recognize the importance of achieving results—funding results-oriented programs, regardless of whether or not they're faith-based or not.

And for those of you who have set the example, I want to thank you very much, but the truth of the matter is, that a recent survey of our Office of Faith-Based and Community Initiatives, headed by [Jim] Towey, of 20 large corporate foundations, found that only about 6 percent of their grants went to faith-based groups. I believe the results are better than that. I am confident that the faith community is achieving unbelievable successes in—throughout our country.

And therefore, I would urge our corporate foundations to reach beyond the norm, to look for those social entrepreneurs who have been—haven't been recognized heretofore, to continue to find people that are running programs that are making a significant difference in people's lives.

When we studied 50 large foundations, we found that one in five prohibited faith organizations from receiving funding for social service programs. In other words, there's a prohibition against funding faith programs from certain foundations in the country. I would hope they would revisit their charters. I would hope they'd take a look at achieving social objectives—make the priority the achievement of certain social objectives before they would make the decision to exclude some who are achieving incredible progress on behalf of our country.

A Role to Play

I believe all of us, no matter what level of government we're in—federal, state, and local—and I believe all of us, no matter if we're private or pubic, ought to allow religious organizations to compete for funding on an equal basis, not for the sake of faith, but for the sake of results. . . .

Government has got a role to play. As you know, this has been quite a controversial subject here in the United States Congress. We believe in separation of church and state—the church shouldn't be the state and the state shouldn't be the church. No question that's a vital part of the country, and that's a vital part of our heritage and we intend to keep it that way. But when it comes to social service funding, the use of taxpayers' money, I think we're able to meet the admonition of separation of church and state and, at the same time, recognize that faith programs provide an important model of success. They help us achieve certain objectives in our country.

It used to be that groups were prohibited from receiving any federal funding whatsoever because they had a cross or a star or a crescent on the wall. And that's changed, for the better. It's changed for the better for those who hurt in our society. And so now, when the government is making social service grants, money is rewarded to groups—awarded to groups that get the best results, regarded of whether they're a faith-based program or not. That's all people want. They want access to grant money on an equal basis, on a competitive basis, so there's no discrimination one way or the other.

I repeat to you, and I'm going to say this about five times, I'm sure: Our job in government is to set goals and to focus on results. If you're addicted to alcohol, if a faith program is able to get you off alcohol, we ought to say, hallelujah and thanks, at the federal level.

Making Progress

One of the things I asked old Jim Towey to do was to let me know if we're making any progress. You know, a lot of people around the country say, politicians are good at talking, but sometimes they don't really follow through. It's kind of like, the check is in the mail. So I said, why don't you give us a score card, and I want to share with you some of the results that has taken place over [2005]. The federal government awarded more than $2.1 billion in competitive social service grants to faith-based organizations [in 2005]. That's an increase of 7 percent over the previous year, and that is 11 percent of all federal competitive social service grants. We're making progress about creating a level playing field for people to be comfortable in, one, applying for grants, and two, when receiving a grant—and then actually getting the money out the door to social service organizations.

For example, $780 million in grants was distributed through the Department of Health and Human Services. USAID [United States Agency for National Development] gave $591 million worth of grants. These are the faith-based organizations—$521 million through HUD [Department of

Housing and Urban Development]. And so going from ground zero to today, we're making progress. I can tell you why, it's because we're measuring.

A lot of people were nervous about applying for grants. I can understand that, you know. They said, why in the world would I want to interface with the federal government? They may try to run my business. They may want to try to tell me how to conduct—how to run my program. We've done a good job I think through these different faith-based offices and throughout our government of assuring people in the government, don't—look, don't tell people how to run their business, accept the way they are, and focus on results. And part of the reason we had these conventions and these outreaches, regional outreaches, is to assure people that the role of the government is to fund, not to micromanage how you run your programs. I repeat to you, you can't be a faith-based program if you don't practice your faith.

We've launched some other initiatives which some of you are involved with—programs to help those who are addicted find treatment. We've talked about mentors for children of prisoners. And for those of you involved in the mentoring program for children of prisoners, I want to thank you on behalf of a grateful nation. You are providing a fantastic service to help make sure the future is bright.

Can you imagine what it would be like growing up with your mom or dad in prison? Maybe some of you have. It's got to be a heartbreaking experience. And a lot of these kids just cry for love. And to help find a loving soul who is willing to embrace a child and to stay with that child is a wonderful contribution to the country, and it makes sense for the federal government to provide funding for such programs.

We are helping prisoners transition back into society. We want to help small service organizations gain capabilities. One of the things that some of you who have been involved with the faith-based community understand, that, you know, the

The Positive Linkage

Whatever direction [President George W. Bush's] faith-based agenda takes, the national debate over the ability of religion to overcome social ills will continue. At stake are not only constitutional issues, but the integrity of America's religious institutions. All the more reason for policy makers to get their facts right. Some of the arguments against allowing religious groups a wider role in helping the poor reveal an astonishing ignorance of what these ministries actually do. Al McGeehan, mayor of Holland, Mich., puts it bluntly: "If people don't understand the positive linkage between faith-based organizations and city hall, they're not living in the real world." Most Americans seem to understand the connection. According to a recent Gallup Poll, nearly 70 percent of those surveyed believe religious organizations do the best job of helping youth in the community.

Joseph Loconte and Lia Fantuzzo,
"Churches, Charity, and Children:
How Religious Organizations Are Reaching
America's At-Risk Kids," 2002. www.religionandsocialpolicy.org.

big guys get rolling and kind of get a nice head of steam up, and there doesn't seem to be much focus on smaller organizations, some of which are just getting started. Our job is to make sure that the Compassion Fund helps startups. I don't want to sound like a business guy, but there are some people just getting started; they need tutoring, they need help. But they can provide a vital service.

One reason faith programs exist is because some good soul sees there's a demand. And they may not be the well-established organization, and it seems like to me it's a proper use of resource to help startups, new social entrepreneurs, small social entrepreneurs get their feet on the ground to provide compassionate help, alongside the big ones. There you go.

There's other targeted programs, as well as social service competitive grant money. And I'm sure you're being briefed on—I hope you're being briefed on all this during this conference. You ought to feel comfortable about making sure that your program has a chance to participate in a myriad of opportunities. We want you to do that. We welcome your participation. We want involvement.

Changing the Culture in Washington

The other thing that we're trying to work hard is to change the culture here in Washington. The faith-based program is relatively new, and it takes a while for cultures to change, and we want people throughout the bureaucracies to not fear the involvement of faith programs and community-based programs in the compassionate delivery of help. And one of the real challenges we have is at the state and local governmental level. We've made good progress, by the way, here at the federal level, on competitive grant money.

See, a lot of money that comes out of Washington is formula-driven. It just kind of flows out. And so sometimes that money goes to the states, and the states are the decision-makers as to whether or not a faith program can be involved in the—in receiving that money to help meet social objectives. We are constantly working with governors and mayors to convince them that having a faith-based office in their respective centers of responsibility will really help improve their state, as well as the—as well as their cities.

And there's progress being made there. I think there's something like 30 governors have now got faith-based offices, and over a hundred mayors have got faith-based offices. And to the extent that you can influence your mayor or your governor, convince them to open up an office and make sure that some of the federal money that flows to the states is open for competitive bidding for faith-based programs.

By the way, we just set up a new faith-based and community office in the Department of Homeland Security. [In February 2006] I signed a bill extending what's called charitable choice; it's a mechanism by which these programs can go forward. And it's—one of the most important things about the legislation I signed, it allows faith-based groups to receive federal funding without changing their hiring practices. This is going to stay around for another five years. In other words, the bill extended the life of the charitable choice provision in the welfare reform law by another five years.

I would hope Congress would recognize the importance of charitable choice and extend it forever. I mean, if it makes sense today, it makes sense forever. . . .

"[I]t is becoming increasingly clear that the Faith-Based Initiative erodes faith in government while also corrupting religion and ill-serving the most vulnerable among us."

Federally Supported Faith-Based Charitable Organizations Should Not Promote Religion

Richard B. Katskee

Richard B. Katskee is assistant legal director of Americans United for the Separation of Church and State. In the following viewpoint, Katskee argues that efforts to fund more faith-based social service providers threatens the balance of religion and government. According to Katskee, religious organizations receiving federal funds formerly agreed not to hire or fire based on spiritual beliefs, provide services to recipients regardless of faith, and allow them to accept or decline religious instruction. However, the author states that the new initiative eliminates this agreement, diverting funds from experienced religious organizations that

Richard B. Katskee, "Paying for Praying: What's Wrong with the Faith-Based Initiative?" *Human Rights*, vol. 33, Summer 2006, pp. 4–5. Copyright © 2006, American Bar Association. All rights reserved. Reproduced by permission.

provide services on a nondiscriminatory basis and funneling them to organizations that favor their followers.

As you read, consider the following questions:

1. According to the author, what "license" does Bush's initiative give to faith-based charitable organizations?
2. As stated by Katskee, what did the Government Accounting Office recently report about federal agencies and faith-based funding?
3. In Katskee's opinion, how do the incentives created by the initiative affect faith-based charitable organizations?

Religious organizations have always been essential to the support network for the least well-off in American society. So what could be wrong with a government program that makes more money available to the soup kitchens, homeless shelters, and substance-abuse-treatment programs that they provide? When it comes to President George W. Bush's Faith-Based and Community Initiatives, the answer, sadly, is . . . quite a lot. Indeed, the Faith-Based Initiative is a case study for what goes awry when we dole out public money without regard for the constitutionally mandated separation of church and state.

Historically, religiously affiliated social-service providers made a simple choice. They could accept public funding and, in exchange, agree to deliver their charitable services as a secular organization would; or they could finance their charitable works entirely through private contributions, and run their programs as they pleased. Those choosing to accept government money—including such well-respected organizations as Catholic Charities, Lutheran Social Services, Jewish Family Services, and Habitat for Humanity—typically formed Section 501(c)(3) nonprofit corporations; made employment decisions based on merit rather than religious affiliation; helped all who demonstrated need according to neutral, secular criteria; and provided services without exacting religious obedience as the price for receiving a benefit. Those choosing instead to limit themselves to private funding remained free to commingle contributions with church assets; to hire and fire based on religious criteria; to provide services only to people of their own faith; and to condition a free meal or a bed for the night on the recipient's willingness to accept religious instruction.

Blurring the Line

But in an effort to increase the number of faith-based social-service providers, the Bush administration has blurred the line between public and private, telling religious groups that they no longer need to choose between religious programming and public funding. Five years into this new system, it is becoming increasingly clear that the Faith-Based Initiative erodes faith in government while also corrupting religion and ill-serving the most vulnerable among us.

One of the most disturbing aspects of the initiative is that, under it, the federal government funds employment discrimination. A special exemption from Title VII (the federal law addressing employment discrimination) allows churches to hire and fire employees—even those without religious duties—based solely on whether, or how well, they adhere to the employers' tenets of faith. The Bush administration has extended this exemption to all faith-based organizations—even those supported entirely by public money—thus giving them license to require applicants to pass religious tests or sign religious oaths to hold government-funded jobs.

What should be equally troubling is the lack of public oversight of faith-based organizations. The federal government now makes grants directly to houses of worship and unincorporated associations that do not file the federal tax returns that ordinary nonprofit entities must. Thus, the government essentially exempts grantees from the critical safeguard of public accountability for use of public funds. And al-

Faith-Based Programs Are Not a Panacea

Just because a program is faith-based does not necessarily mean that it is run well or is capable of providing everything that a person in need requires. The next stage of welfare reform will require decentralized delivery of support services to those now off welfare but still not integrated into our labor force. Those services should be configured by a wide array of community and faith-based groups, but the programs should be evaluated by their performance, not by their faith.

Stephen Goldsmith, "A Little Help from Above,"
Wall Street Journal, *January 30, 2001. www.opinionjournal.com.*

though the U.S. Constitution forbids using tax dollars for inherently religious activities or discriminatory programs, the Government Accountability Office recently reported that federal agencies have done such a poor job drafting regulations on the use of faith-based funding, and such a poor job monitoring compliance, that many grant recipients routinely violate the constitutional strictures and offer federally funded benefits to the needy on a pray-for-pay basis.

Nor do religious institutions fare any better under the Faith-Based Initiative. Nearly 400 years ago, Roger Williams, the Baptist leader who founded Rhode Island, warned that religious freedom would flourish only if religious institutions could choose their own precepts and priorities, and decide how best to pursue them, without governmental interference. But with taxpayer dollars now up for grabs, those institutions have substantial incentives to reorder their priorities—and perhaps even to distort the tenets of their faith—to increase their share of the spoils. The result is that they begin to cede important aspects of church governance to administrative agencies and officials whose preferences determine where the public dollars will flow.

The Biggest Losers

The biggest losers of all under the Faith-Based Initiative are those whom the public funds were meant to help. Rather than making more money available to private social-service providers, the Faith-Based Initiative simply diverts government funds from the secular and religious organizations that for decades have used them to provide quality care to people of all faiths, now directing the money to less-experienced groups, many of which are also uninterested in reaching out to religiously diverse populations. When government shifts funds from organizations providing services on a nondiscriminatory basis to those favoring people who share their beliefs, members of minority faiths (whose religious institutions are least likely to compete successfully for government dollars) and the nonreligious are often left without reasonable options for obtaining badly needed services. In a nation founded on religious freedom, no one should have to submit to unwanted religious instruction or coerced prayer in order to receive the hot meal or medical care that taxpayer dollars provide.

James Madison and Thomas Jefferson, the architects of the First Amendment principle of church-state separation, warned that if religion became intermingled with government, both would suffer. One need look no further than the Faith-Based Initiative to see how prophetic that warning was. If the real motivation for this initiative is to recognize the value of religious institutions in serving the least well-off in American society, would we not do better to follow the path that Jefferson and Madison charted, letting institutions perform their charitable works as they see fit—free from the corrupting influences that come with the promise of easy public money—while ensuring that our tax dollars provide benefits to people of all faiths on equal terms?

> "[T]he Ten Commandments are a foun-
> dation of rule and law, and a symbol
> of the role that religion played, and
> continues to play, in our system of gov-
> ernment."

Posting the Ten Commandments in Public Areas Is Constitutional

Antonin Scalia

*In the following viewpoint excerpted from his dissenting opinion
in* McCreary County, Kentucky v. *American Civil Liberties
Union of Kentucky (2005), Antonin Scalia argues that displaying the Ten Commandments on public and government property
is constitutional and does not advance one religious view over
others. According to the author, the Ten Commandments widely
represent the core teachings of Christianity, Judaism and Islam.
Scalia also states that its display, in a historical context as a
document, is secular and that similar displays and references are
well-documented, endure at all levels of government today and
have not been prohibited or deemed unconstitutional. Scalia is
an associate justice of the U.S. Supreme Court.*

Antonin Scalia, dissenting opinion, *McCreary County, Kentucky, et al. v. American Civil
Liberties Union of Kentucky et al. U.S. Supreme Court, Certiorari to the United States
Court of Appeals for the Sixth Circuit,* Findlaw.com, June 27, 2005.

As you read, consider the following questions:

1. What examples does Scalia give as evidence for prayer in American history?
2. In Scalia's view, how does the government currently "improve the position of religion"?
3. In the Foundations Displays that included the Ten Commandments, in what manner were the documents exhibited, according to the author?

On September 11, 2001, I was attending in Rome, Italy, an international conference of judges and lawyers, principally from Europe and the United States. That night and the next morning virtually all of the participants watched, in their hotel rooms, the address to the Nation by the President of the United States concerning the murderous attacks upon the Twin Towers and the Pentagon, in which thousands of Americans had been killed. The address ended, as Presidential addresses often do, with the prayer "God bless America." The next afternoon I was approached by one of the judges from a European country, who, after extending his profound condolences for my country's loss, sadly observed "How I wish that the Head of State of my country, at a similar time of national tragedy and distress, could conclude his address 'God bless _____.' It is of course absolutely forbidden."

That is one model of the relationship between church and state—a model spread across Europe by the armies of Napoleon, and reflected in the Constitution of France, which begins "France is [a] . . . secular . . . Republic." France Const., Art. 1, in 7 Constitutions of the Countries of the World, p. 1 (G. Flanz ed. 2000). Religion is to be strictly excluded from the public forum. This is not, and never was, the model adopted by America. George Washington added to the form of Presidential oath prescribed by Art. II, § 1, cl. 8, of the Constitution, the concluding words "so help me God." The Supreme Court under John Marshall opened its sessions with the prayer,

"God save the United States and this Honorable Court." The First Congress instituted the practice of beginning its legislative sessions with a prayer. The same week that Congress submitted the Establishment Clause as part of the Bill of Rights for ratification by the States, it enacted legislation providing for paid chaplains in the House and Senate. The day after the First Amendment was proposed, the same Congress that had proposed it requested the President to proclaim "a day of public thanksgiving and prayer, to be observed, by acknowledging, with grateful hearts, the many and signal favours of Almighty God." President Washington offered the first Thanksgiving Proclamation shortly thereafter, devoting November 26, 1789 on behalf of the American people "'to the service of that great and glorious Being who is the beneficent author of all the good that is, that was, or that will be,'" thus beginning a tradition of offering gratitude to God that continues today. The same Congress also reenacted the Northwest Territory Ordinance of 1787, 1 Stat. 50, Article III of which provided: "Religion, morality, and knowledge, being necessary to good government and the happiness of mankind, schools and the means of education shall forever be encouraged." And of course the First Amendment itself accords religion (and no other manner of belief) special constitutional protection.

Actions by the Founders Reflected Beliefs

These actions of our First President and Congress and the Marshall Court were not idiosyncratic; they reflected the beliefs of the period. Those who wrote the Constitution believed that morality was essential to the well-being of society and that encouragement of religion was the best way to foster morality. The "fact that the Founding Fathers believed devotedly that there was a God and that the unalienable rights of man were rooted in Him is clearly evidenced in their writings, from the Mayflower Compact to the Constitution itself" [*School Dist. of Abington Township v. Schempp* (1963)]. President Washington opened his Presidency with a prayer, and reminded his fellow citizens at the conclusion of it that "reason and experience both forbid us to expect that National morality can prevail in exclusion of religious principle." President John Adams wrote to the Massachusetts Militia, "we have no government armed with power capable of contending with human passions unbridled by morality and religion. . . . Our Constitution was made only for a moral and religious people. It is wholly inadequate to the government of any other." Thomas Jefferson concluded his second inaugural address by inviting his audience to pray:

> "I shall need, too, the favor of that Being in whose hands we are, who led our fathers, as Israel of old, from their native land and planted them in a country flowing with all the necessaries and comforts of life; who has covered our infancy with His providence and our riper years with His wisdom and power and to whose goodness I ask you to join in supplications with me that He will so enlighten the minds of your servants, guide their councils, and prosper their measures that whatsoever they do shall result in your good, and shall secure to you the peace, friendship, and approbation of all nations."

Nor have the views of our people on this matter significantly changed. Presidents continue to conclude the Presidential oath with the words "so help me God." Our legislatures, state and national, continue to open their sessions with prayer led by official chaplains. The sessions of this Court continue to open with the prayer "God save the United States and this Honorable Court." Invocation of the Almighty by our public figures, at all levels of government, remains commonplace. Our coinage bears the motto "IN GOD WE TRUST." And our Pledge of Allegiance contains the acknowledgment that we are a Nation "under God." As one of our Supreme Court opinions rightly observed, "We are a religious people whose institutions presuppose a Supreme Being" [*Zorach v. Clauson* (1952)].

With all of this reality (and much more) staring it in the face, how can the Court *possibly* assert that "'the First Amendment mandates governmental neutrality between . . . religion and nonreligion,'" and that "[m]anifesting a purpose to favor . . . adherence to religion generally," is unconstitutional? Who says so? Surely not the words of the Constitution. Surely not the history and traditions that reflect our society's constant understanding of those words. Surely not even the current sense of our society, recently reflected in an Act of Congress adopted *unanimously* by the Senate and with only 5 nays in the House of Representatives, criticizing a Court of Appeals opinion that had held "under God" in the Pledge of Allegiance unconstitutional. Nothing stands behind the Court's assertion that governmental affirmation of the society's belief in God is unconstitutional except the Court's own say-so, citing as support only the unsubstantiated say-so of earlier Courts going back no farther than the mid-20th century. And it is, moreover, a thoroughly discredited say-so. It is discredited, to begin with, because a majority of the Justices on the current Court (including at least one Member of today's majority) have, in separate opinions, repudiated the brain-spun "*Lemon* test" [established in *Lemon v. Kurtzman* (1971)] that embodies the supposed principle of neutrality between religion and irreligion. And it is discredited because the Court has not had the courage (or the foolhardiness) to apply the neutrality principle consistently. . . .

I have cataloged elsewhere the variety of circumstances in which this Court—even *after* its embrace of *Lemon's* stated prohibition of such behavior—has approved government action "undertaken with the specific intention of improving the position of religion." Suffice it to say here that when the government relieves churches from the obligation to pay property taxes, when it allows students to absent themselves from public school to take religious classes, and when it exempts religious organizations from generally applicable prohibitions of religious discrimination, it surely means to bestow a benefit on religious practice—but we have approved it. Indeed, we have even approved (post-*Lemon*) government-led prayer to God. In *Marsh v. Chambers*, the Court upheld the Nebraska State Legislature's practice of paying a chaplain to lead it in prayer at the opening of legislative sessions. The Court explained that "[t]o invoke Divine guidance on a public body entrusted with making the laws is not . . . an 'establishment' of religion or a step toward establishment; it is simply a tolerable acknowledgment of beliefs widely held among the people of this country." (Why, one wonders, is not respect for the Ten Commandments a tolerable acknowledgment of beliefs widely held among the people of this country?) . . .

Broad and Diverse

Besides appealing to the demonstrably false principle that the government cannot favor religion over irreligion, today's opinion suggests that the posting of the Ten Commandments violates the principle that the government cannot favor one religion over another. That is indeed a valid principle where public aid or assistance to religion is concerned, or where the free exercise of religion is at issue, but it necessarily applies in a more limited sense to public acknowledgment of the Creator. If religion in the public forum had to be entirely nondenominational, there could be no religion in the public forum at all. One cannot say the word "God," or "the Almighty," one cannot offer public supplication or thanksgiving, without contradicting the beliefs of some people that there are many gods, or that God or the gods pay no attention to human affairs. With respect to public acknowledgment of religious belief, it is entirely clear from our Nation's historical practices that the Establishment Clause permits this disregard of polytheists and believers in unconcerned deities, just as it permits the disregard of devout atheists. The Thanksgiving Proclamation issued by George Washington at the instance of the First Con-

gress was scrupulously nondenominational—but it was monotheistic. In *Marsh v. Chambers*, we said that the fact the particular prayers offered in the Nebraska Legislature were "in the Judeo-Christian tradition," posed no additional problem, because "there is no indication that the prayer opportunity has been exploited to proselytize or advance any one, or to disparage any other, faith or belief."

Historical practices thus demonstrate that there is a distance between the acknowledgment of a single Creator and the establishment of a religion. The former is, as *Marsh v. Chambers* put it, "a tolerable acknowledgment of beliefs widely held among the people of this country." The three most popular religions in the United States, Christianity, Judaism, and Islam—which combined account for 97.7 percent of all believers—are monotheistic. All of them, moreover (Islam included), believe that the Ten Commandments were given by God to Moses, and are divine prescriptions for a virtuous life. Publicly honoring the Ten Commandments is thus indistinguishable, insofar as discriminating against other religions is concerned, from publicly honoring God. Both practices are recognized across such a broad and diverse range of the population—from Christians to Muslims—that they cannot be reasonably understood as a government endorsement of a particular religious viewpoint. . . .

A Significant Role

To any person who happened to walk down the hallway of the McCreary or Pulaski County Courthouse during the roughly nine months when the Foundations Displays were exhibited, the displays must have seemed unremarkable—if indeed they were noticed at all. The walls of both courthouses were already lined with historical documents and other assorted portraits; each Foundations Display was exhibited in the same format as these other displays and nothing in the record suggests that either County took steps to give it greater prominence.

Entitled "The Foundations of American Law and Government Display," each display consisted of nine equally sized documents: the original version of the Magna Carta, the Declaration of Independence, the Bill of Rights, the Star Spangled Banner, the Mayflower Compact of 1620, a picture of Lady Justice, the National Motto of the United States ("In God We Trust"), the Preamble to the Kentucky Constitution, and the Ten Commandments. The displays did not emphasize any of the nine documents in any way: The frame holding the Ten Commandments was of the same size and had the same appearance as that which held each of the other documents.

Posted with the documents was a plaque, identifying the display, and explaining that it "contains documents that played a significant role in the foundation of our system of law and government." The explanation related to the Ten Commandments was third in the list of nine and did not serve to distinguish it from the other documents. It stated:

> "The Ten Commandments have profoundly influenced the formation of Western legal thought and the formation of our country. That influence is clearly seen in the Declaration of Independence, which declared that, 'We hold these truths to be self-evident, that all men are created equal, that they are endowed by their Creator with certain unalienable Rights, that among these are Life, Liberty, and the pursuit of Happiness.' The Ten Commandments provide the moral background of the Declaration of Independence and the foundation of our legal tradition."

On its face, the Foundations Displays manifested the purely secular purpose that the Counties asserted before the District Court: "to display documents that played a significant role in the foundation of our system of law and government." That the Displays included the Ten Commandments did not transform their apparent secular purpose into one of impermissible advocacy for Judeo-Christian beliefs. Even an isolated display of the Decalogue conveys, at worst, "an equivocal message, perhaps of respect for Judaism, for religion in general, or for law." But when the Ten Commandments appear alongside other documents of secular significance in a display devoted to the foundations of American law and government, the context communicates that the Ten Commandments are included, not to teach their binding nature as a religious text, but to show their unique contribution to the development of the legal system. This is doubly true when the display is introduced by a document that informs passersby that it "contains documents that played a significant role in the foundation of our system of law and government."

The same result follows if the Ten Commandments display is viewed in light of the government practices that this Court has countenanced in the past. The acknowledgment of the contribution that religion in general, and the Ten Commandments in particular, have made to our Nation's legal and governmental heritage is surely no more of a step towards establishment of religion than was the practice of legislative prayer we approved in *Marsh v. Chambers*, (1983), and it seems to be on par with the inclusion of a crèche or a menorah in a "Holiday" display that incorporates other secular symbols. The parallels between this case and *Marsh* and *Lynch* [*Lynch v. Donnelly* (1984)] are sufficiently compelling that they ought to decide this case, even under the Court's misguided Establishment Clause jurisprudence.

Acknowledgment of the contribution that religion has made to our Nation's legal and governmental heritage partakes of a centuries-old tradition. Members of this Court have themselves often detailed the degree to which religious belief pervaded the National Government during the founding era. Display of the Ten Commandments is well within the mainstream of this practice of acknowledgment. Federal, State, and local governments across the Nation have engaged in such display. The Supreme Court Building itself includes depictions of Moses with the Ten Commandments in the Courtroom and on the east pediment of the building, and symbols of the Ten Commandments "adorn the metal gates lining the north and south sides of the Courtroom as well as the doors leading into the Courtroom." Similar depictions of the Decalogue appear on public buildings and monuments throughout our Nation's Capital. The frequency of these displays testifies to the popular understanding that the Ten Commandments are a foundation of the rule of law, and a symbol of the role that religion played, and continues to play, in our system of government. . . .

Not Advancing Any One Faith

The Court has in the past prohibited government actions that "proselytize or advance any one, or . . . disparage any other, faith or belief," or that apply some level of coercion (though I and others have disagreed about the form that coercion must take). The passive display of the Ten Commandments, even standing alone, does not begin to do either. What Justice Kennedy said of the crèche in *Allegheny County* [*Allegheny County v. ACLU* (1989)] is equally true of the Counties' original Ten Commandments displays:

> "No one was compelled to observe or participate in any religious ceremony or activity. [T]he count[ies] [did not] contribut[e] significant amounts of tax money to serve the cause of one religious faith. [The Ten Commandments] are purely passive symbols of [the religious foundation for many of our laws and governmental institutions]. Passersby who disagree with the message conveyed by th[e] displays are free to ignore them, or even to turn their backs, just as they are free to do when they disagree with any other form of government speech."

Nor is it the case that a solo display of the Ten Commandments advances any one faith. They are assuredly a religious symbol, but they are not so closely associated with a single religious belief that their display can reasonably be understood as preferring one religious sect over another. The Ten Commandments are recognized by Judaism, Christianity, and Islam alike as divinely given. . . .

In sum: The first displays did not necessarily evidence an intent to further religious practice; nor did the second displays, or the resolutions authorizing them; and there is in any event no basis for attributing whatever intent motivated the first and second displays to the third. Given the presumption of regularity that always accompanies our review of official action, the Court has identified no evidence of a purpose to advance religion in a way that is inconsistent with our cases. The Court may well be correct in identifying the third displays as the fruit of a desire to display the Ten Commandments, but neither our cases nor our history support its assertion that such a desire renders the fruit poisonous.

"[T]he posting of any one version of the Ten Commandments endorses certain religious denominations to the exclusion of others. . . ."

Posting the Ten Commandments in Public Areas Is Unconstitutional

Jacob Rolls

In the following viewpoint, Jacob Rolls alleges that displaying the Ten Commandments on public or government property is unconstitutional if the display has a religious purpose, produces an effect that advances or inhibits religion, or creates an excessive involvement with religion. For example, Rolls claims that two Supreme Court cases—in which Ten Commandments displays were exhibited on state property, courthouse grounds, and school classrooms—overstepped at least one of these criteria. Also, the author rejects the argument that the Ten Commandments represents the diverse religious values of Christianity, Judaism, and Islam. Rolls is a 2004 graduate of American University's Washington College of Law.

Jacob Rolls, "Why Ten Commandments Displays on Government Property Are Unconstitutional," *The Humanist*, vol. 65, March-April 2005, pp. 12–17. Copyright © 2005 American Humanist Association. Reproduced by permission.

As you read, consider the following questions:

1. According to Rolls, what documents were exhibited in the "courthouse version" of the Kentucky Ten Commandments display?

2. In the author's view, how was the display in *Van Orden* a "sham" for religious purposes?

3. How does Rolls counter the argument that the phrase "In God We Trust" on U.S. currency legitimizes religious texts on public or government property?

On December 13, 2004, seventeen national religious and secular organizations filed a joint friend of the court brief to the U.S. Supreme Court addressing the two Ten Commandments cases the Court is scheduled to begin hearing March 2, 2005, with a ruling expected sometime in the fall. . . .

The first case, *Thomas Van Orden v. Texas Governor Rick Perry*, deals with whether a six-foot-tall red granite monument depicting the Ten Commandments, erected on the grounds of the state capital of Texas, is an unconstitutional attempt to establish state sponsored religion. The second case, *McCreary County v. American Civil Liberties Union of Kentucky*, involves the "Foundations of Law" displays in the McCreary and Pulaski county courthouses that include the Ten Commandments alongside nine historical and legal documents as a "sampling of documents that influenced American law and government." . . .

Since maintaining separation of church and state is vital to a free society, it's important to review the arguments set forth by the brief and see how they work to preserve fairness and liberty.

The Establishment Clause

As civil libertarians are aware, the First Amendment begins with the words "Congress shall make no law respecting an establishment of religion, or prohibiting the free exercise thereof." These two outwardly competitive mandates are referred to as the establishment clause and the free exercise clause, respectively. Aside from their unelaborated text, no further guidance was offered by the framers to instruct the government on how to undertake the difficult task of protecting religious freedoms while simultaneously ensuring government neutrality.

Since 1971, however, U.S. courts have used the test developed out of the Court's decision in *Lemon v. Kurtzman* as the paramount guiding framework to determine whether government conduct is constitutional under the establishment clause. Under what is called the *Lemon* test, as originally formulated, reviewing courts are required to consider three important points: whether the government activity in question has a secular purpose, whether the activity's primary effect advances or inhibits religion, and whether the activity fosters an excessive entanglement with religion. In these cases, the AHA [American Humanist Association] brief argues that the first and second prongs of the *Lemon* test are violated by the Ten Commandments displays in both Kentucky and Texas. Essentially what this means is that the facts demonstrate that the government posted the Ten Commandments primarily for religious reasons and that the effect of posting them in the manner done has the primary effect of advancing religion. Indeed, the thrust of the brief's argument is that, because of both a constitutionally impermissible "purpose" and "effect" under *Lemon*, the Court should declare these government actions unconstitutional.

While it may seem that the government has clearly acted outside the scope of *Lemon*, however, there is always a chance that the Court could change the rules of the game. One of the issues it will decide with these cases is whether the *Lemon* framework should continue to even be used to decide establishment cases. Church-state separation proponents argue that *Lemon* provides a workable and dynamic approach because it embodies all of the values for which the establishment clause stands. I mention this now because the rest of this article—like the bulk of the brief—assumes that the Court will stay with the *Lemon* test in its analysis, thus making it clear that the state actors in Kentucky and Texas violated the establishment clause by posting the Ten Commandments in the way they did.

With respect to the public posting of the Ten Commandments, the Supreme Court has only decided one case that is "directly on point." In 1981 it held in *Stone v. Graham* that posting the Ten Commandments on classroom walls was unconstitutional because the purpose for posting them was plainly religious, despite the fact that the defendants had offered the claim that the Ten Commandments were the "fundamental legal code of Western civilization." As will be discussed below, this is conceptually identical to some of the purposes currently offered. *Stone* does not, however, state that it is never okay to post the Ten Commandments in schoolrooms, or anywhere else for that matter. Rather, the Court ruled that "an appropriate study of history, civilization, ethics, comparative religion, or the like" could render their posting constitutional and it's likely that this "exception" will be key to deciding whether or not the practices at issue in the current cases violate the establishment clause. . . .

Case Backgrounds

In *McCreary* the issue is the posting of the Ten Commandments on Kentucky county courthouse grounds and in school classrooms. In this case, the Ten Commandments were posted and reposted three times during the course of the litigation in an effort to make them constitutionally permissible. The first time, they were displayed alone and weren't part of "larger educational, historical, or retrospective exhibits." The second time, the commandments were surrounded by the complete text of other items (such as the national motto "In God We

Trust") and by excerpts from others that specifically celebrated religion (such as a proclamation by President Ronald Reagan designating 1983 as the "Year of the Bible"). After being ordered by the Sixth District Circuit Court to immediately remove these modified displays and refrain from erecting any similar ones in the future, the Kentucky authorities posted a third version. The new "courthouse version" included the entire "Star Spangled Banner," Declaration of Independence, Mayflower Compact, Bill of Rights, Magna Carta, National Motto, Preamble to the Kentucky Constitution, Ten Commandments, a statue of Lady Justice, and a one-page prefatory document entitled "The Foundations of American Law and Government Display." The new "schoolhouse version" included all of these documents (aside from the prefatory document) and the school board resolution allowing the commandments to be displayed.

The third versions of the displays contain the Kentucky authorities' most recent "formal" or proffered justifications for posting the Ten Commandments. . . .

The district court found that all of the modified displays violated the Constitution and ordered their removal.

Van Orden v. Perry is different from *McCreary* in a couple of ways. In this case, the Ten Commandments are displayed on a single granite monument that stands six feet tall and three and a half feet wide. It—like hundreds of other such monuments displayed on public property around the country—was a gift from the Fraternal Order of Eagles. Texas accepted this particular monument in 1961 and placed it on the capital grounds. In addition to the Ten Commandments text, the monument contains several symbols that are etched into it. These include an eye inside a pyramid, closely resembling the symbol displayed on the one-dollar bill; two Stars of David; depictions of two tablets with ancient Hebrew script; a symbol representing Christ (made up of two Greek letters, Chi and Rho, superimposed on each other); and an American eagle grasping the American flag. Just below the text of the commandments, the monument bears the inscription: "Presented to the People and Youth of Texas by the Fraternal Order of Eagles of Texas 1961."

The purported purpose for posting this monument was to "recognize and commend a private organization for its efforts to reduce juvenile delinquency." In 1993, several years after the purported secular purpose was offered, the monument was repositioned on the direct line between the legislative chambers, the executive office of the governor, and the Supreme Court to continue "to reflect the role of the Commandments in the making of law." Unlike the Sixth Circuit Court in *McCreary*, here the Fifth Circuit determined that the Ten Commandments monument is constitutional under *Lemon* and it has allowed it to remain on the capital grounds.

The Religious Intent of the Government's Position

In order to decide whether the government activity in question has a predominantly secular purpose under *Lemon*, the courts have had to decipher "sham" secular purposes from "sincere" ones by employing comprehensive examinations of proffered and actual purposes. This analysis itself is at issue now, as is shown by the Court's framing of the issues it will be deciding. The Court will rule on whether "a prior display by the government in a courthouse containing the Ten Commandments that was enjoined by a court permanently taints and thereby precludes any future display by the same government when the subsequent display articulates a secular purpose and where the Ten Commandments is a minority among numerous other secular historical documents and symbols."

But even the most cursory analysis of the content, context, and history of the displays at issue shows that the government's proffered secular purposes are a sham and that religious purposes predominate. In *Van Orden*, the desire to "commend an

Battlegrounds over Religion

Proposals to post the Ten Commandments often create wide divisions in communities that are already struggling with profound problems of their own. Opponents of these initiatives—many of whom are deeply religious themselves—are portrayed as being anti-religious freedom or even anti-God. School board meetings and local elections have become battlegrounds over religion rather than over practical issues such as juvenile crime and low test scores.

When an Illinois school board voted unanimously to post the Ten Commandments in public schools, the resulting controversy dominated local politics for months. After several months of acrimonious debate, the school board rescinded the decision in order to avoid a costly lawsuit.

Anti-Defamation League, "The Ten Commandments Controversy: A First Amendment Perspective," 2008. www.adl.org.

organization for its work to combat juvenile delinquency" is shown to be a sham because, although it's an outwardly secular interest, it's accomplished by religious means. At best this makes the government's proffered purpose constitutionally suspect, especially in light of the plainly religious (specifically monotheistic) nature of the Ten Commandments. Also, it's important to consider the government's stated purpose for relocating the monument to "reflect the role of the Commandments in the making of law" as indicative of their true purposes. This relocation has no connection whatsoever to the original supposed effort to honor a private organization and constitutes further evidence of the religious motivations for erecting and maintaining the display on public property in the first place.

In *McCreary* it's undisputed that the original purpose was religious. It wasn't until correctly ordered by the Sixth District Court to remove the displays that the government suggested it was trying to show that the Ten Commandments provide the "moral background of our Declaration of Independence" and "the foundation of American law and government." As stated before, this is conceptually identical to the outwardly secular assertions of purpose that were rejected by the Supreme Court in *Stone*. Beyond this clear evidence of religious motivation, however, the final modified displays reveal that the government failed even to exert an effort to educate citizens about the purported civic, legal, or historical value of the Ten Commandments. All that it did was—without any historical proof, substantiated commentary, or plausible support—display the religious text among other documents that do have civic or patriotic value. These non-efforts shouldn't qualify for the Court's approval as "an appropriate study of history, civilization, ethics, comparative religion, or the like."

The larger reason that these displays shouldn't qualify as "an appropriate study" is that the government's purported historical purposes are difficult or impossible to effectuate given what is known about U.S. history. The most fundamental expressions of the American system of government—the Declaration of Independence, the Constitution, and the Bill of Rights—all explicitly reject the religious ideology propounded in the Ten Commandments. Thomas Jefferson, the author of the Declaration of Independence, rejected claims that Christianity influenced the common law. It's also understood that the reference to God in the Declaration of Independence didn't refer to the God who gave Moses the Ten Commandments but, rather, to the "watchmaker" God of eighteenth-century deism. Furthermore, the Constitution and the Bill of Rights reject the encroachment of religious influence even more strongly than the Declaration does. Neither even mentions God, let alone refers to the Ten Commandments. Furthermore, the first four commandments (of most versions of the Decalogue) would plainly violate the Constitution because the state can't prohibit idolatry, the worship of other gods, or blasphemy—nor can it mandate respect for the Sabbath—without violating the First Amendment's establishment, free exercise, or free speech clauses. . . .

Posting the Ten Commandments Advances Religion

In order to determine whether a government action has the primary effect of advancing religion, the courts ask whether an objective observer (or a "reasonable person") would perceive the action as a state endorsement of religion. This part of the *Lemon* test is designed to find out whether the government has conveyed a message that a religion is favored, preferred, or promoted over other beliefs. In addition to the government's failure to integrate the Ten Commandments displays into an appropriate educational curriculum, as noted above, there are several things that would lead a reasonable person to conclude that these displays constitute state endorsement of a specific faith.

All of the displays at issue involve the Ten Commandments being interwoven with secular objects and placed on public property that is necessarily used by theists and nontheists alike. Rather than neutralizing the religious impact of the Ten Commandments, as the government suggests, this conveys the message that Christian and Jewish religious messages have a community value equal to civic and patriotic messages and that the government endorses those religious messages just as it does the civic and patriotic messages. For instance, in *Van Orden* there is an etching of a bald eagle gripping an American Flag right above the Ten Commandments. This specifically links religion and civil government (without any explanation of the alleged links between religion and civil government, which could arguably save the display under

Stone). Also, the monument is located within the vicinity of secular historical monuments, further increasing the likelihood that a reasonable person might believe that the state is endorsing the religious message embodied in the monument. This same problem is apparent in *McCreary*, where the Ten Commandments are displayed with several secular documents without being successfully integrated into their secular subject matter.

For the reasonable person, the perception of government endorsement isn't ameliorated by the fact that the displays were privately funded because "the mere posting of the copies under the auspices of the legislature provides the official support of the State" under *Stone*. And from a logical standpoint, how could one suggest that the essence of a foundational article of faith for Christian and Jewish adherents could somehow be rendered religiously neutral by allowing a private individual or entity to finance its display?

Then there is the matter of the government acting to endorse one religion over another or to endorse religion generally. Both the establishment clause and the "effects" prong of the *Lemon* test exist to prevent the government in a pluralistic society from doing this. Government posting of the Ten Commandments on public grounds constitutes a government endorsement of certain religious sects to the exclusion of religious minorities and nontheists—and the posting of any one version of the Ten Commandments endorses certain religious denominations to the exclusion of others that rely on materially different versions of the commandments.

The exclusion of religious minorities and nontheists is apparent upon a reading of the first line of the Ten Commandments, which states, "I am the Lord thy God," and which illustrates both the monotheistic and the sectarian character of the displays. Similarly, because there are at least five different versions of the commandments, not to mention variant translations and abridgements, the posting of any one of them to the exclusion of the others indicates that the government is exercising an unconstitutional denominational preference. It not only infringes upon the sectarian differences among various Christian denominations that were central to the origins of our republic but it also conveys the message from the state that the Protestant version is "correct" and the Muslim, Jewish, and Catholic versions aren't. It is precisely for reasons such as these that the Constitution's drafters enacted the First Amendment and why the U.S. government should avoid giving its imprimatur to any version of the Ten Commandments. . . .

Where promoters of government support for religion are concerned, little things have a way of becoming big things. Each small action in this direction is used to justify the next larger action. Thus the legal appearance of "In God we trust" on currency has been applied as an argument toward legitimizing those same words being posted in courthouses and public schools. By the same token, it can be expected that if a Ten Commandments monument can be placed on government property then a Ten Commandments lesson can be mandated in the public school curriculum and perhaps even a reference to the Ten Commandments added to the Pledge of Allegiance. Over time this process could result in the virtual establishment of religion, potentially leading to a theocratic state, one of the very things the First Amendment was written to prevent. Thus church-state activists work to nip every such effort in the bud.

Periodical Bibliography

The following articles have been selected to supplement the diverse views presented in this chapter.

Mark Ambinder	"Republicans and Evangelicals," *Weekly Standard*, September 18, 2006.
The Economist	"The Lesson from America," November 3, 2007.
Mike Elkin	"The Closing of the Church Door," *Newsweek International*, May 19, 2008.
Frances Fitzgerald	"The New Evangelicals," *New Yorker*, June 30, 2008.
Michael Gaynor	"The Constitution, *Stare Decisis*, and the Ten Commandments," *RenewAmerica*, August 4, 2005.
Leadership	"Body Politic," Summer 2008.
Doug MacManaman	"A Note on Separation of Church and State," *Catholic Insight*, April 2007.
Jon O'Brien	"A True Balancing Act: Religion, Reproduction, and Public Policy," *Conscience*, Winter 2007.
Chris Roberts	"The Story of the Decalogue: Why Putting the Ten Commandments on Public Property Is Unbiblical," *National Catholic Reporter*, May 20, 2005.
Jacob Rolls	"Why the Ten Commandments on Public Property Are Unconstitutional," *Humanist*, March–April 2005.
Jim Towey	"The Faith-Based Initiative: Compassion in Action," *Human Rights*, Summer 2006.
Michael Sean Winters	"Respecting Religion: Can Politicians Learn the Language of Churchgoers?" *America*, October 13, 2008.

CHAPTER 3

Does Technology Threaten Privacy?

Chapter Preface

In August 2007, the American passport went electronic—embedded on its back cover is a radio frequency identification (RFID) chip. Smaller than a human hair is wide, the chip contains the same data on the passport's identification page and is capable of storing biometric identifiers, or unique physical characteristics such as fingerprints, iris scans, and facial features. Currently, the digital image of the passport bearer's face serves as a biometric identifier used by face recognition technology. Electronic passports can be instantaneously "read" by a specially designed chip reader without contact, and digital signature technology—which is used in credit cards—authenticates the data.

Advocates claim that electronic passports have several benefits: They automate identity verification at immigration checkpoints and thwart passport theft, tampering, and counterfeiting. According to Angela Aggeler, former spokesperson for the State Department's Bureau of Consular Affairs, "A U.S. passport is one of the most valuable documents in the world," adding that, "the harder we make it for someone to fake a passport or travel as an impostor on a U.S. passport, the better off and safer we all are." Addressing fears that data stored in electronic passports can be stolen and used for identity theft, Martin McCourt, an executive for RFID technology vendor Gemalto, claims, "Even if someone could copy the information on your e-passport chip, it doesn't achieve anything because all of the information is locked together in such a way that it can't be changed. It's no different than someone stealing your electronic passport and trying to use it."

Critics, on the contrary, argue that electronic passports do not enhance security and actually increase the vulnerability of national borders. In August 2008, British newspaper the *Times* reported that during its own tests, electronic passports implanted with digital images of a suicide bomber and Osama bin Laden bypassed chip reader software used by a United Nations agency. Others contend that the current technology of electronic passports will become obsolete before the documents expire, endangering the travelers who carry them. Security technology expert Bruce Schneier states, "The security mechanisms on your passport chip have to last the lifetime of your passport. It is as ridiculous to think that passport security will remain secure for that long as it would be to think that you won't see another security update for Microsoft Windows in that time."

Electronic passports are but one of numerous technological developments adopted by federal, state, and local governments intended to enhance the security of the United States and its citizens. In the following chapter, the authors discuss how emerging technologies may offer higher levels of protection, or conversely, open new threats to privacy.

| "Our privacy is shrinking quicker than the polar ice cap; technology is eroding it faster than the legal system can protect it."

Technology Threatens Privacy

David H. Holtzman

In the following viewpoint, David H. Holtzman contends that digital technology has placed privacy in jeopardy. From e-mails to medical tests to purchases, Holtzman argues that every human transaction is being stored. He also warns that personal electronics and hidden radio frequency identification (RFID) tags constantly track the people who own them, and computerized sensors, surveillance cameras, and face-recognition technologies capture their every move. Furthermore, the author predicts that the loss of privacy may culminate into the loss of free thinking in a fear-driven society. Holtzman is a security and technology expert, and author of Privacy Lost: How Technology Is Endangering Your Privacy.

As you read, consider the following questions:

1. What, according to Holtzman, is a "digital Doppelgänger"?

2. Why does the author insist that bodily and medical privacy is threatened?

3. In Holtzman's view, how does the decreasing price of digital technology increase its threat to privacy?

Privacy is a universally cherished prerogative that isn't much of a right at all. Few laws protect our seclusion, and they weaken every year. Our privacy is shrinking quicker than the polar ice cap; technology is eroding it faster than the legal system can protect it. This trend cannot be reversed in any obvious way. Privacy, as we know it today, is lost.

At its most basic level, privacy is about information control—who owns knowledge about us? The German term *informationelle Selbstbestimmung*, which means "informational self-determination," suggests that we control our own information. But today our information has slipped out of our control, and as a result we have lost our privacy. This loss has been caused by the most significant society-impacting science of our generation—computerized technology. My intention in writing this book is to explain the connection between technology and privacy and to speculate about where things might be headed.

This book is not written just for privacy advocates or for technologists, however. Rather, it's for all who are disturbed about the growing amount of data available on them, about who's doing the collecting, and about what the collectors are going to do with all that personal information. It's also for those who are concerned about the growing number of exceedingly well-publicized privacy violations and who are wondering how many other incidents haven't become public. It's hard not to notice the unending stream of news stories describing one egregious privacy violation after another: companies losing the financial information of millions of customers, a civil servant in the U.S. Department of Veterans Affairs having a laptop stolen that contained personal information on nearly every American who's ever served in the military, a Boston newspaper wrapping papers in printouts of its customers' credit-card numbers. These stories are all documented and discussed in the book. They are, in themselves, a testament to the effect of technology on our privacy.

Privacy Lost is also for people who get nervous about privacy-hostile government actions like the Patriot Act. These counterterrorist programs give millions of government agents a get-out-of-jail-free card, permitting electronic probing of U.S. citizens on a scale that would have made even J. Edgar Hoover blush. None of these government activities would be possible without the availability of sophisticated information technology like data mining, which is used to sift through the rapidly growing data heaps of our newly digital civilization.

Our data include our e-mails, photographs, medical results, travels, and purchases. Eventually every transaction will be stored somewhere digitally and therefore will be accessible to a persistent searcher. As a rule of thumb, according to Moore's Law, digital storage devices get twice as powerful every eighteen months for the same price. However, the cost of human labor stays the same. Therefore, it's cheaper to buy additional disks than to figure out what to delete. Digital data never disappear, and searching technology like Google is good enough that all information will be found. Like Poe's raven, our past may come back to haunt us when we least expect it. It's no coincidence that e-mails have been the key evidence at the center of most political and financial scandals since the mid-1990s. Data last forever. Privacy does not.

The digital universe parallels the one we live in, except it's littered with lost and forgotten information, data, and facts—a silicon twilight zone. Each of us has a twin in this universe, a digital Doppelgänger that reflects our lives and experiences and will be around when we're long gone. This electronic simulacrum shares our birth date and Social Security number and all our specifics: what we've bought, where we've traveled, the state of our health. Even though we may zealously guard our personal information, our double will tell anyone about us because that electronic twin is not under our control.

It's impossible to walk through this modern world without leaving behind indelible footprints in its silicon sand. Most financial activities, for example, leave a digital imprint somewhere because a record of every cashless transaction goes into someone's database. A whole industry has sprung up around selling and storing personal information about our behavior and activities. Each bit seems innocuous, but, in aggregate, this electronic montage provides a frighteningly detailed history of what we do, when and where we do it, and whom we do it with. As you'll read about later in the book, computer software is also beginning to make some good guesses as to what we think. Do we want new laws protecting our privacy from these intrusions, or are we willing to put up with them to have a better shopping experience?

We are also being tracked by our gadgets, such as cell phones (even when they're off) and Geographic Positioning Systems in our cars. A new technology called Radio Frequency Identification enables small chips to be hidden in packages, books, and even clothes. These little devices know essential information about us and can be surreptitiously interrogated from thirty feet away. Soon this technology will be prevalent in our lives. Are we willing to live without our gadgets if we know that they erode our privacy?

In addition, we're under constant observation by computerized sensors. In most modern cities our picture is snapped dozens of times a day by surveillance cameras. License-plate-reading and face-recognition programs are matching these pictures to names. So far, the worst result of this capability is the automatic issuing of speeding tickets but additional uses will be developed. Will we ever get used to being watched twenty-four hours a day?

Even our bodies are being tagged, analyzed, and stored for future cross-reference. A simple cheek swab or drop of blood is enough to analyze our DNA, which indicates our tendency to inherit certain health problems. Health care providers and employers would naturally like to screen out those of us with genetic problems to keep down the overall cost of medical coverage. As a result, our genetic road map sometimes makes it difficult to get insurance or even a job. Several U.S. states and some nations are also building sweeping databases of citizens' DNA information for future use. Are we as a nation okay with a genetically biased health care system?

Some of these capabilities have been available for years, but weren't threatening because they were too expensive to be widely deployed on a large scale. Unfortunately digital technology is now cheap, very cheap—and it is getting more so every year. The best protection against wholesale privacy abuse has always been the cost. However, this fiscal barrier is effective only against physical, not virtual, items because the economics are different in the digital world. For example the profitability point for spam (junk email), regardless of the volume, is insanely low compared with the break-even point for postal mail because the incremental cost per item of spam is close to zero. The cost of a postage stamp is a natural brake on the proliferation of junk mail. There's no equivalent friction for e-mail. America Online (AOL) has instituted a program called Good Mail, which, purports to cut back on spam by charging mass e-mailers who want to send to AOL recipients. The theory is that the payments will deter spammers. Are we willing to pay for all our e-mail in the future, or is spam a nuisance that we are willing to put up with for free stuff?

Our lives are represented electronically in databases across the world. The decentralization of this information makes it difficult to regulate. These computerized storehouses are necessary for so many business and governmental purposes that

The Danger of RFID Tags

Imagine: The Gap links your sweater's RFID [radio frequency identification] tag with the credit card you used to buy it and recognizes you by name when you return. Grocery stores flash ads on wall-sized screens based on your spending patterns, just like in [the film] *Minority Report*. Police gain a trendy method of constant, cradle-to-grave surveillance.

You can imagine nightmare legal scenarios that don't involve the cops. Future divorce cases could involve one party seeking a subpoena for RFID logs—to prove that a spouse was in a certain location at a certain time. Future burglars could canvass alleys with RFID detectors, looking for RFID tags on discarded packaging that indicates expensive electronic gear is nearby. In all of these scenarios, the ability to remain anonymous is eroded.

Declan McCullagh,
"RFID Tags: Big Brother in Small Packages,"
January 13, 2003. http://news.cnet.com.

most people do not view them as a threat. And the political climate is not favorable for changing the situation. These information tools are seen as important weapons in our nation's arsenal. We live in a turbulent time. All but the most snugly bundled liberties have been whipped by the wind of fear that has blown through the United States since the attacks on the World Trade Center and the Pentagon in 2001. The natural balance between national security and privacy has tipped precariously toward security. Are we as citizens in a democracy willing to grant our government indefinite powers to anonymously invade our privacy if it makes us safer? What if we only think it makes us safer? Should government be limited in what it can see and do with the information it collects on us?

But it's not just government tracking citizens. Every group that uses computers incrementally erodes the privacy of its constituents when it starts keeping lists. The newspapers are full of privacy-related stories, ranging from abuses of the Patriot Act to President George W. Bush's authorization of possibly illegal domestic surveillance. Every few weeks, we hear about massive data breaches caused by careless data handling by private companies, while others, like Google, are holding enormous amounts of personal information—so much so that the government is trying to forcibly get access to it. The privacy situation in the United States and Canada is at an Orange Alert level and will not be going back to Yellow again in my lifetime.

Information gathering is the new arms race. Superior knowledge gives the knower the ability to predict what's going to happen. And a lot of money can be made from predicting the future. Governments collect personal information to spot subversion. Merchandisers use it to target or persuade consumers. Financial institutions assess creditworthiness. Politicians find donors. Terrorists hatch plots. This fungible information is easily transportable and can be converted into cash in any currency in the world. You often hear the old legend that our body is worth $4.50, stripped for parts. Our digital identity is worth far more than that. Information about us is worth $20–$50 to a business trying to sell us a product and is worth many thousands of dollars to an identity thief.

Our ethical sense is not yet fine-tuned to the changes brought about in the privacy arena by technology. Nor is our legal system. Western society views the universe through the lens of science. In this model, technological progress is ideologically pure and apolitical. Information is just data, just facts. We find it hard to accept the idea that knowledge can be dangerous. We don't have a cultural perspective that supports this idea, unlike people living under repressive regimes, who know that information, true or not, can get them jailed or even killed. This intellectual blind spot, refusing to believe that control of information should be regulated, is one of the major reasons why the United States has no comprehensive privacy laws today.

This book is different from other books about privacy because it's centered on technology, not the law. In this century, technology moves fast and sets the pace for social issues, leaving the law lagging behind. Legislation works best when fixing a problem that has clearly definable boundaries. However, information technology itself and the ways in which it's harvested and sold are developing at such a rapid rate that new laws are likely to address technology that industry has already abandoned. Congress has historically done a miserable job at providing protection against future problems, even the slow-moving ones. These kinds of problems cannot be resolved in Congress, just as they cannot be fixed solely in the courts. The law will always lag behind the technology.

Privacy legislation has also been difficult to enact because the damages from privacy loss are not clearly understood. To many people, privacy issues are linked to immediate annoyances, like telemarketing phone calls. Because the consequences are not directly apparent, the hardest situations to regulate in a democratic society are those, like smoking or environmental protection or control of information, that cause long-term damages.

Privacy Lost is divided into six parts. The first part is about the damages caused by the loss, including what I call the Seven Sins Against Privacy. The second part reviews some of the history behind our concept of privacy, how related technology has evolved, and how new technology leads to new invasions of privacy. The third part discusses the context of privacy; it includes a chapter on the legal basis on the United States, another on how privacy relates to identity, and a third on how the idea of privacy varies culturally. The fourth part deals with the mechanics of snooping, databases, surveillance, and networking technologies. The fifth part describes the snoopers themselves, the marketing companies and the government. The last part suggests some ways you can slow or staunch your loss of privacy. The Recommended Reading list at the end of the book provides suggestions for further reading on the topics covered.

Throughout the book you'll find numerous stories and examples, culled from newspapers, magazines, and the Internet, about how privacy invasions hurt people. Although privacy violations happen to celebrities more often they affect normal people, the ones who mistakenly think that the government or the law is protecting them. If you take one idea away from reading this book, it should be that you have the right to control information about yourself. Even if the law doesn't recognize this right, you should. Privacy is, in a legal and practical sense, based on our expectations. Even though Americans have no explicit constitutional right to privacy, most think that we do. People are constantly surprised that there is no mention of privacy in the Constitution. Government is, in fact, powerless to regulate the availability and flow of personal information; even more dangerously it believes it can. This book discusses some steps individuals can take to protect themselves instead of relying on the government.

Polls indicate that people are willing to give up their privacy in exchange for safety. However, the damage caused by the loss of privacy could reach into other areas of our lives as well. For instance, the ability to keep our thoughts and opinions to ourselves gives us the freedom to exercise our other rights without fear of retribution. Privacy allows us to peacefully exercise other rights such as freedom of speech and religion and the right to bear arms. The answer to the question of who controls information about us touches many other areas such as intellectual property and genetic engineering. It may be the most important domestic policy question of this century.

A long-term danger to society resulting from a total loss of privacy protection is that our creative and freethinking culture could be replaced by one that rewards fear-driven mediocrity. It happened on a smaller scale in Hollywood after the Senator Joseph McCarthy hearings and was part of daily life in the Puritan colonies. Those who know that they're watched don't call attention to themselves, and thus they disappear. The economic might of Western innovation cannot be sustained by a nation of ghosts.

"*Technology has created major new privacy challenges, and at the same time, technology also provides the tools to address them.*"

Technology Should Not Be Blamed for All Privacy Threats

Michael Turner

In the following viewpoint, Michael Turner emphasizes personal accountability in privacy and technology issues. Turner asserts that many people have adopted the use of the Internet, personal computers, and other technologies without taking precautions to guard private information. Thus, Turner suggests that three important issues must be addressed to support electronic privacy: awareness of protecting personal information from the inappropriate use of technology, advocacy for corporations to use and keep such data safe, and encouragement of government to keep privacy protection legislation and regulations up-to-date. Turner is a member of the city of Ottawa, Canada's Task Force on eGovernment.

Michael Turner, "Privacy and Technology Conference—Panel Discussion: Privacy and Technology: Enhancing Privacy or Not?" *Riley Information Services*, March 31, 2008. www.rileyis.com. Reproduced by permission.

As you read, consider the following questions:

1. How does the author respond to the claim that "security doesn't equal privacy"?
2. According to the author, for whom are technology's privacy risks "quite small"?
3. What is part of the solution, in Turner's view?

To ask if technology enhances privacy is somewhat akin to asking if taxes enhance public services. The two are inextricably intertwined—technology has created major new privacy challenges, and at the same time, technology also provides the tools to address them.

But the difficulty is that many of us are too quick to learn how to use these slick new technologies while too slow to learn how to protect ourselves from those who are interested in our information, which these days means our identity.

Too many of us don't understand the risks we run every day when using our office or home computers. Too many of us don't know how to take the necessary precautions to block outside access to our systems, to ensure private information remains so. Frankly, this is because personal computers and the Internet are still relatively new and immature technologies, and weren't originally designed with privacy and security in mind. This will change, but it will take another five to ten years.

Security and Privacy

In fact, it's already changing quite quickly. But not fast enough to protect many of us. I might add that, already today, I've heard two speakers declare that security doesn't equal privacy. Very true—but without security, your chances of privacy are much diminished.

Too quickly for comfort, the term "hacker" has gone from meaning a computer enthusiast who improves and customizes a software program, to the nerdy teenager who figures out how to read your personal files from next door, to the organized crime professionals in another country trying to break into the big corporate systems that hold the information you've passed on to them in the course of normal transactions.

The public is nervous and leery of giving out too much information as a result. And rightly so, with credit card and other personal data freely offered for sale in private "chat rooms" frequented by nasty people using the Internet to enrich themselves at our expense. But unfortunately, these matters are often beyond our personal control, and it's often the organizations that should be protecting our private information most carefully who seem instead to be the most careless.

I'm sure you've all heard about the incredible case of TJX, the U.S. parent company of well known firms such as Winners, Home Sense, and TJ Maxx. From mid-2005 until the end of 2006, their systems were routinely broken into and a record of somewhere between 50 and 90 *million* credit card and debit card records were stolen! These card numbers with the holder's information were then sold to numerous other criminal organizations. This theft broke the previous record for sheer size of the theft, cost the company many hundreds of millions of dollars, cost credit card companies millions more, and brought into sharp relief the way in which colossal mismanagement of private information by a company not even based here in Canada can affect millions of Canadians.

In the United States, the Federal Trade Commission estimates that roughly 10 million Americans have their personal information pilfered and misused in some way or another every year, costing consumers $5 billion and businesses $48 billion annually. The figures from Canada are considerably lower, not just because we're a tenth the size, but because so much of our private data in the hands of commercial companies is actually held in the United States and may not always be captured in the Canadian numbers.

The "Double-Edged Sword" Reality

On a much smaller scale, most of us have received fake e-mails trying to lure you into a fake Web site made to look like your bank or perhaps department store, in an attempt to convince you that you need to enter your personal or financial information as part of some records verification or update procedure. This is usually referred to as "phishing"—technology used to trick the unwary, one at a time.

But it's not just computer and Internet technology that is used in this way, so let's not be too quick to blame the technology for all our privacy problems. What about the strange calls we encounter occasionally when someone phones claiming to be with your bank attempts to get you to willingly volunteer your personal and financial information. Not so much technological engineering as social engineering, but with the same affect.

Or the midnight recycling collector, who sorts through your personal papers at the curb looking for personal info that can be used to manufacture new documents, and "borrow" your identity for criminal purposes. Not the direct result of technology, but one more approach helping make identity theft the fastest growing crime of the new century.

Most of these examples are related to the "double-edged sword" reality of how technology not only brings amazing benefits, but new risks. Though, for those of us who take the simple technical precautions of preventing easy access to our computers and data, the risks are really quite small—except when dealing with "corporate idiocracy", such as in the TJX case!

Of much greater concern to me from a privacy concern is the manner in which governments in the United States, Canada, the U.K. [United Kingdom] and other countries are

Research Is Underway to Enhance Privacy Technologies

New privacy-related consumer products appear in the marketplace all the time. These products include software to clean up files left behind on a computer by Web browsers and e-mail programs, and privacy related features in security products. Software designed to block adult Web site content from children includes privacy-related features that can prevent children from providing personal information to Web sites.

A promising new area of privacy enhancing technologies that has not yet come to market are tools to de-identify information in databases. These include tools to selectively scrub data so that just enough data is removed to insure that it is non-identifiable (including removing entries that might identify an individual because they describe characteristics that are likely unique to that individual). In addition, research is underway on techniques for adding randomness to data before it is added to a database in such a way that individual data is not reliable but aggregate data remains useful.

Lorrie Faith Cranor,
"The Role of Privacy-Enhancing Technologies," 2005.
www.cdt.org.

now claiming the right to search my laptop when I cross the border into these countries. They claim it's "just another container", but I may have sensitive business or financial information on it.

Not to mention the problem created by the U.S. "Patriot Act", which permits American authorities to demand access to any information held by a U.S. based company, and makes it illegal for that company to even tell us that the U.S. government has been looking at my information. And while you may think your information is safe and sound, held and managed by a *Canadian* company, do you really know where your data is tonight, and who it's out with?

I'm also very concerned at the manner in which commercial information aggregators like Doubleclick, PointClick, and others who use millions of Web transactions and site visits, combined with data mining from other sources, to build detailed personal profiles that can be sold to other companies wanting to sell to you. And there's also a continued proliferation of semilegal and even illegal "spyware" which companies try to install on your machine when you visit a Web site, to learn exactly what sites you visit, which pages, for how long, and so on. The only difference between this type of commercial spyware and spyware that attempts to harvest passwords and credit card numbers is the purpose to which the information is put.

Part of the solution will no doubt be in the increasing sophistication of the technologies supporting on-line security, including machine to machine authentication, as well as personal authentication of the users, with accompanying processes to allow us to better control user access to data systems. You'll be hearing more of this in the coming months and years, usually in the form of acronyms such as IEAA—which is shorthand for Identification, Enrollment, Authentication and Authorization. Or EA&A—which stands for Enrollment, Authentication and Authorization, and "Triple A" applications—which refers to Authentication, Authorization and Accounting systems.

Challenge and Promise

Watch as well for continued discussion on the challenges and promise of new biometric technologies for authentication, including the creation of "pseudobiometric passwords", new technologies for spotting outside attempts to break into data systems and for preventing damage by limiting the machine to only predefined acceptable actions, as well as new "autonomic" systems, which are self-healing when damaged or when they fail.

Unfortunately, you can also count on new technology enabled privacy threats in the coming years. For example, inexpensive high definition video cameras, which transmit their data back to central monitoring posts by low cost wireless data links, will make video surveillance much easier to afford and install. Newly developed password "cracker" programs will now allow the more sophisticated hacker parked outside your home or a commercial building to break into the store's or home's network within minutes, no matter whether you've carefully encrypted the wireless router signals or not. And as high tech crime continues to become a global activity of organized crime, data theft programs downloaded from casual visits to compromised Internet sites are becoming increasingly hard to detect, let alone block.

Yes indeed—not entirely cheerful news. But there will certainly be plenty of issues for those concerned with personal and corporate privacy, and plenty of challenges for those concerned with technology security, not to mention with law enforcement and international organized crime. But let me wrap up by suggesting we can segment the discussion . . . into, perhaps, three basic questions:

1. Are we adequately aware of how to protect our personal and private information from deliberate theft through inappropriate use of technology, and how to respond if we find ourselves a victim? And,

2. Are we doing enough to ensure that corporate entities using the new technologies to gather and hold our personal information for business reasons are held accountable for collecting and holding only what is essential and for keeping that data safe? And,

3. Are we doing enough to encourage our politicians and government officials to keep our rudimentary privacy protection legislation and regulations up-to-date, so that we're not constantly finding ourselves "behind the curve" and defenceless as technologies continue to rapidly evolve?

"Skeptics' concern centers on fundamental social issues that sound all too Orwellian: the loss of privacy and the erosion of social trust."

Public Surveillance Cameras Violate Privacy

Laurent Belsie

In the following viewpoint, Laurent Belsie alleges that, despite the now widespread use of surveillance cameras for security purposes, some skeptics believe that the cameras violate privacy rights. The skeptics believe that surveillance cameras also contribute to the erosion of social trust, in that people would rather put up a camera for security purposes than simply trust their neighbors. Several other important issues pertaining to surveillance cameras are who should have access to the information gathered by these cameras and if the cameras really help to deter crime and terrorism. Laurent Belsie is a staff writer for The Christian Science Monitor.

As you read, consider the following questions:

1. According to Bill Brown, what amendment does the use of surveillance cameras violate?

2. What is one example of a controversial situation that is cited by the article as a reason why traffic cameras are not necessarily a good thing?

3. How many surveillance cameras is Britain estimated to use?

Standing on a traffic island in the middle of Times Square, Bill Brown might as well be on stage.

TV cameras sweep the street to film lead-ins for news shows; security cameras protect store entrances; Web cameras focus out on the street so tourists can wave to friends and family back home via the Internet. Since the devices are often hidden or disguised, it takes several seconds for his small tour group to pick them out.

On a suspected police camera that hangs overhead, Mr. Brown slaps on a "You are being watched" sticker and defiantly reads the Fourth Amendment of the United States Constitution: "The right of the people to be secure in their persons, houses, papers, and effects, against unreasonable searches and seizures, shall not be violated, and no warrants shall issue, but upon probable cause. . . ."

The Skeptics' Case

Score a small and purely symbolic victory for one of the biggest underdog movements in America. Even as homeowners gleefully wire up their homes with inexpensive Web cams, even as employers put up closed-circuit TV and cities install surveillance equipment on everything from traffic intersections to school buses, a small group of skeptics is beginning to question the effects of all this technology.

Of course, after recent terrorist attacks and sniper shootings, those leading the backlash risk being drowned out by catcalls from an edgy public. On the other hand, they're tapping into deep pools of public suspicion about surveillance.

On the face of things, the new invasion of electronic eyes looks different from George Orwell's nightmare. It comes mostly from private sources, not government.

But skeptics' concern centers on fundamental social issues that sound all too Orwellian: the loss of privacy and the erosion of social trust.

They ask: Will you trust your neighbor in the 21st century? Or in putting up a security camera—just to make sure—are we somehow pulling out an essential thread of the social fabric?

"It seems that we indeed trust no one," writes William Staples in his recent book, *Everyday Surveillance*. "'Just put up the camera,' [authorities] say, and the problems will go away. In the case of the school bus, for example, once the camera is in place, no one has to bother teaching children *why* they should behave, it's enough just to get them to do it. This begs the question, how will they act when they are not under the gaze of the camera?"

The Expansion of Surveillance Cameras

No one knows how many surveillance cameras sweep public space in the United States, but experts agree the number is rising. Sales of closed-circuit TV systems grew faster last year [2001] than those of any other electronic security product, according to a dealer survey by Security Sales & Integration magazine in Torrance, Calif. Here in Times Square, perhaps the nation's most monitored public area, the number of cameras has more than tripled in four years, according to Brown, to 258 from 75.

Another reason for the expansion: falling costs. "I don't think people realize how easy it is—and cheap—to buy a camera, put it on the Internet, and watch," says Michael Naimark, another skeptic of video surveillance. "I am concerned that we're going to put up large-scale surveillance [systems] too quickly."

That's why, as a kind of civil-disobedience manual for the electronic age, he has published "How to ZAP a Camera." The Internet report details his experiments with lasers and cameras in Japan. Using something as simple as a laser pointer, he has temporarily disabled video cameras.

One unaffiliated website actually carries directions on ways to destroy and disable cameras. Another site from an art, technology, and activism collective called the Institute for Applied Autonomy allows users to find "routes of least surveillance" through Manhattan.

Who Has Access, Who Has Control?

Mr. Naimark's point, however, is to force people to think more deeply about the social effects of security cameras and, peacefully, to register their protest. "It's not so much a case of surveillance cameras as who has access to them, who controls representation" of individuals, such as merging a photo of someone's face with a photo of someone else's body, he says. "I don't think there are simple answers."

Take traffic cameras, the kind that snap photos of cars running red lights. The technology captures license-plate numbers, and then motorists get tickets by mail. By some accounts, the system makes intersections safer.

In five of six California cities that installed the cameras, for example, the number of traffic accidents fell between 3 percent and 21 percent, according to a state auditor's report this summer [2002]. When California stopped using its traffic cameras, accidents at intersections went back up. That's why a rising number of jurisdictions are turning to the technology. Last month [October 2002], Raleigh, N.C., approved deployment of cameras at 15 intersections.

The cameras will not only deter red-light runners but also keep offenders honest, says Benson Kirkman, the city council's mayor pro tem. When a car ran a red light and sideswiped him 20 years ago, the driver initially apologized, then claimed the light was green once an eyewitness left the scene. With a camera, such high jinks wouldn't work, Mr. Kirkman argues.

Nevertheless, the technology has run into controversy. A retired woman in nearby Chapel Hill, N.C., got a $50 ticket for running a red light in Fayetteville, N.C., even though she'd never visited that city. San Diego suspended its program after residents complained the private contractor running the program was overzealous. The city has since started paying the contractor a flat fee, rather than a portion of each ticket generated.

Government Regulations

But a hodgepodge of state laws is only beginning to catch up with the technology.

Washington State is now pushing to toughen its standards after the state supreme court ruled, to many people's astonishment, that videotaping up women's skirts in a mall did not violate the state voyeurism statute.

Even operators of approved video cameras may be using the technology to ogle women or capture images of actions that, while legal, are compromising, critics say.

"As things stand now there's no federal law against video cameras. There are no guidelines in place about what can be done with the images," complains Donna Lieberman, executive director of the New York Civil Liberties Union. "We run the risk of technology running amok and putting people's entire lives on film."

There are other sides to the equation, of course. For one thing, Big Brother isn't lurking around the corner. "We're not being watched by some conspiratorial government, we're watching each other," says Ken Goldberg, a professor of operational engineering at the University of California at Berkeley and author of *Beyond Webcams* a book on remotely guided robots. The surge in surveillance "definitely is going to erode some elements of privacy and increase elements of paranoia

that go with that. On the other hand, having the control in the hands of private individuals may be a good thing."

Last month, Mr. Goldberg wired his own house with off-the-shelf security cameras. "Hopefully, it will act as a deterrent," he says. "Is that so bad? I don't think so."

Neither do many other people in these uncertain times. Since the Sept. 11 [2001] attacks, camera surveillance has been on the upswing around the world, according to a recent joint report by London-based Privacy International and the Electronic Privacy Information Center in Washington.

And public outcry has been muted.

In Britain, the developed world's leader in video surveillance, many residents have accepted, even welcomed, the technology. One study, catalogued by a crime-reduction charity in London called Nacro, found that even when Britons were fed a series of antisurveillance questions, they still supported cameras by 56 percent. When fed prosurveillance questions, support tipped 91 percent.

Diminishing Returns on Deterring Crime

How much cameras really deter crime remains an open question. When the Scottish Centre for Criminology studied their effect on two communities, it found crime fell in the small town but rose in the large city (Glasgow). Nacro also found mixed results. The technology seems to have a lifecycle, the charity found, initially reducing crime but often with diminishing effect as time went on.

And they reinforce discrimination in Britain—a key concern among US civil-liberties groups. The Nacro study found the cameras disproportionately target men, particularly black men.

"They are indiscriminately surveilling people," says Brown, who—besides counting cameras and giving surveillance tours—also directs the New York Surveillance Camera Players. Since 1996, the group has staged various plays in front of surveillance cameras. Sometimes the actors exorcise the technology; sometimes they pray to it, all to raise the issue in a kind of dramatic protest.

Will the US follow in Britain's footsteps? As wired as this country is, it has nowhere near Britain's ratio of cameras to people. With less than one-quarter of America's population, Britain has an estimated 1.5 million surveillance cameras (some reports suggest 2.5 million or more). But antisurveillance activists are also realists.

"I can get the subject on the mainstream political agenda, but that's about it," says Brown. "In 50 years I would hope that the movement I am building has won," he adds. If it doesn't, "I fear that New York in 50 years would become a dystopia in a sci-fi way."

"Industry players believe most people
are willing to give up a little privacy, at
least in public, in return for enhanced
security."

Public Surveillance Cameras
Increase Security

John Edwards

*John Edwards is a business technology journalist based near
Phoenix, Arizona. In the following viewpoint, Edwards states
that advancing surveillance video technology is increasing security in public places and businesses. The latest developments, he
claims, allow public surveillance cameras to better detect suspicious situations without the use of facial recognition, license
plate reading, or human operators. The author proposes that
these "intelligent" unmanned cameras can spot potential terrorists, unattended objects, and even identify and track lost children. Also, Edwards suggests that many people may be willing to
trade a bit of public privacy in exchange for more security.*

As you read, consider the following questions:

1. What can the latest surveillance video systems detect in
   real time, as stated by the author?

John Edwards, "The Unblinking Eye," *Electronic Design*, vol. 55, April 27, 2007, pp. 38–
40. Copyright © 2006 Penton Media, Inc. All rights reserved. Reproduced by permission.

2. According to Edwards, what happens when suspicious behavior or objects are detected by the unmanned cameras of SmartCatch?

3. Why does Edwards insist that intelligent video analysis can be a "powerful business tool"?

San Francisco International Airport (SFO) is a hub for business travelers, vacationers, immigrants, stopover passengers, on-site workers—and a whole lot of suspicious-looking people. That's why it's not surprising to discover that the airport operates an extensive video surveillance system. What is surprising is how very smart the system is.

When it comes to video surveillance, people tend to imagine banks of sharp-eyed human observers endlessly scanning video screens for anything out of the ordinary. But that's not necessarily true anymore. Sophisticated video analysis technologies are rapidly replacing people as ever-vigilant sentinels.

"If you have a security guard looking at a monitor, he's probably going to look at it for 10, 20 minutes and then get bored and zone out," says Dilip Sarangan, a security analyst for Frost and Sullivan, a technology market research firm. "A computer never gets bored, and nothing goes unchecked."

By studying human behavior and automatically detecting the presence and absence of various objects in real time, intelligent video analysis promises enhanced security at an overall lower cost. "It's more of a proactive rather than a reactive approach to video surveillance," says T. Jeff Vining, a security industry analyst at Gartner, another technology research firm.

Government agencies and other organizations are scooping up intelligent video analysis products at an accelerating pace. Over a dozen firms now offer some form of the technology. The vendor pool includes companies like Vidient, Westec Interactive, and Visual Defence, all of which offer products that can survey a local area—indoors or outdoors—and spot anything out of the ordinary.

Intelligent video system sales are projected to grow from $60 million in 2005 to $400 million in 2012, Sarangan predicts. "It's heading into the business mainstream," he says.

Scanning SFO

More than 32 million passengers pass through San Francisco International Airport each year. Visually studying even a small percentage of this flood of humanity for quirks and behavior that might betray a sinister motive would require an army of human observers glued to video monitors. For a solution that would prove effective without financially crippling manpower costs, SFO turned to SmartCatch, an intelligent video analysis technology offered by Vidient.

SmartCatch works in conjunction with the airport's existing closed-circuit television (CCTV) systems to detect aberrant or suspicious behavior and distinguish those patterns of activity from normal activities. When the behavior-based software spots an anomaly, it sends a video clip via a pager, laptop, cell phone, or other communications device to a responder, who can then investigate the situation.

"When we say 'behavior,' we don't mean facial recognition or license plate reading. We're really talking about a combination of human and object behaviors," says Steve Goldberg, Vidient's CEO. In other words, the system looks for people and objects, such as suitcases or packages, that aren't in the right place or have lingered in a place for too long.

"So if you parked your car at the curb, where it's only supposed to be for dropoff, and the car doesn't move, it will alert security," says Michael McCarron, SFO's community affairs director. The system also can spot "human tailgating," when two people pass through a secure door on a single ID card swipe, as well as things like crowd formation and people going through an exit lane the wrong way.

Broad Support for Surveillance Cameras		
	Increased use of surveillance cameras	
	Support	Oppose
All	71%	25
Age 18–29	61	33
65+	80	17
Men	66	29
Women	75	21

TAKEN FROM: ABC News/Washington Post Poll: Surveillance Cameras, July 29, 2007.

Vidient's Windows-based technology is based on sophisticated video algorithms developed over three years by NEC's computer vision engineers. "The algorithms are generally based on adaptive filtering or adaptive processing—neural network types that have been used in other data and voice applications," says Goldberg. SmartCatch detects suspicious situations with an accuracy rate between 95 percent and 98 percent, Goldberg notes.

Like most other intelligent video analysis technologies, Vidient's product functions by seeing each image as a mosaic of pixels. The algorithms then work to make sense out of the mosaic's movement, or lack of movement, and to separate the pixel cluster from background clutter. "Basically, video analytics is all software," Sarangan says.

Advancing Technology

Cameras streaming IP video make it relatively easy to add analytic technology to a new or existing surveillance system, says Michael Godfrey, Visual Defence's chief technology officer. Since the raw data is in a digital format already, intelligent video analysis technology can be dropped into the system easily. "I can put my analytic server anywhere within the network," Godfrey says.

Thanks to faster and more powerful processors, it's now possible to build analytic capabilities directly into surveillance cameras. Lumenera, for example, has introduced a series of cameras that use Texas Instruments' DaVinci digital video technology to deliver advanced image processing, compression, and video analytics.

"The cameras themselves are getting more intelligent," Godfrey says. Also, many "smart" cameras now support downloadable analytics modules produced by third-party vendors. This lets system owners use a module designed for a particular task, such as body movement analysis or object tracking. "You're not tied with one specific type," Godfrey notes. Different modules can be distributed to various cameras across the system, wherever a particular capability is needed.

Whether it's camera-based or server-based, analytics has its limits despite these advances. Even the most sophisticated algorithms running on the most powerful processors can have trouble coping with busy, visually complex environments—the types of places authorities most want to monitor.

"If you put it into an urban area, like New York City, there's so much going on at once it's almost like it overloads the brain," Vining says. "But if you have a defined area to monitor, it can work very well." Even so, intelligent video analysis can still be tricked into registering false alerts.

"I might be standing outside the airport waiting for somebody to pick me up," Sarangan says. "It might look like I'm loitering, but I'm not doing anything wrong." Yet system users are generally willing to tolerate the occasional false positive as the price they must pay for not overlooking a possibly serious situation, notes Vining.

Network capacity is another concern. "If you're streaming [video] across the network, it's about 2 Mbytes/s," Sarangan says. That means a system with 100 cameras needs to move nearly 200 Mbytes every second. Since many large-footprint installations like mass transit systems can require thousands of cameras, network costs can quickly mount. "That's a lot of data to be streaming across a network," Sarangan says.

Expanding Market

As intelligent video analysis becomes more widely available at ever lower price points, the technology is filtering down to a wide array of enterprises. "We have seen strong demand for the technology from specialty retailers, jewelry stores, and even supermarkets," says Jon Bolen, chief technology officer of Westec Interactive.

Retailers can use intelligent video analysis to detect shoplifters. Casinos can tap the tools to spot cheaters. And, theme parks often turn to smart cameras to identify and locate lost children.

It could even be a powerful business tool. Stores can judge which floor displays are most popular with shoppers, while fast food restaurants can better assess their staffing needs by monitoring crowd sizes throughout the day.

Industry players believe most people are willing to give up a little privacy, at least in public, in return for enhanced security. Vining believes intelligent video analysis systems are destined to pop up in an ever growing number of public spaces.

"It's what the world is coming to," Vining says.

Periodical Bibliography

The following articles have been selected to supplement the diverse views presented in this chapter.

Joshua Breitbart   "Will Technology Kill Privacy?" *Gotham Gazette*, November 2007.

Clayton Collins   "Anatomy of a Shopper," *Christian Science Monitor*, June 1, 2005.

Louis E. Frenzel   "Location Awareness—Boon or Privacy Bane?" *Electronic Design*, June 29, 2006.

Steven Gray   "Should Schools Fingerprint Your Kids?" *Time*, September 25, 2007.

William Norman Grigg   "Terrorists Chip In," *American Conservative*, February 12, 2007.

Darice M. Grzybowski   "Patient Privacy: The Right to Know Versus the Need to Access," *Health Management Technology*, September 2005.

Erik Larkin   "Electronic Passports May Make Traveling Americans Targets, Critics Say," *PC World*, April 11, 2005.

John McElhenny   "Smile, You're on Security Camera," *Boston Globe*, March 28, 2004.

Mobile Radio Technology   "Same Threats, Different Technology," September 1, 2006.

Marc Rotenberg   "Technology and Privacy: Old Problems and New Challenges," *Human Rights*, Winter 2007.

Julian Sanchez   "The Pinpoint Search: How Super-Accurate Surveillance Technology Threatens Our Privacy," *Reason*, January 2007.

OPPOSING
VIEWPOINTS®
SERIES

How Has the War on Terrorism Affected Civil Liberties?

Chapter Preface

In October 2008, Attorney General Michael Mukasey signed new domestic investigation guidelines into effect for the Federal Bureau of Investigation (FBI), consolidating the five sets of guidelines that separately addressed criminal, national security, civil disorder and demonstration, and foreign intelligence investigations. According to Mukasey and FBI director Robert Mueller in a joint statement, "These guidelines provide more uniform, clearer, and simpler rules for the FBI . . . operations are designed to allow the FBI to become, among other things, a more flexible and adept collector of intelligence."

However, opponents argue that the new guidelines lower the threshold for beginning investigations, opening the door to surveillance and intrusions without clear basis of suspicion. An October 2008 *New York Times* editorial claims that FBI agents now "may engage in lengthy physical surveillance, covertly infiltrate lawful groups, or conduct pretext interviews in which agents lie about their identities while questioning a subject's neighbors, friends, or work colleagues based merely on a generalized 'threat.'" In addition, the American Civil Liberties Union (ACLU) asserts that racial profiling will proliferate. Anthony D. Romero, the ACLU's executive director, states, "The new guidelines provide no safeguards against the FBI's improperly using race and religion as grounds for suspicion. They also fail to sufficiently prevent the government from infiltrating groups whose viewpoints it doesn't like."

Proponents maintain that the new guidelines do not expand the reach of the FBI in excess. Responding to the *New York Times* editorial, Robert Mueller maintains, "[T]he guidelines do not give special agents new powers," adding that "they do extend to the agents investigating terrorists and spies the same long-established—and widely accepted—tools used for decades to investigate bank robbers or mobsters." Mueller also claims that numerous changes result from "unprecedented consultation with Congress and major civil rights and civil liberties groups." For instance, a fact sheet released by the U.S. Department of Justice insists that the new guidelines incorporate "a majority of the suggestions that it received" from these groups.

The consolidation of the FBI's domestic investigation guidelines follows years of governmental actions since the September 11, 2001, terrorist attacks to aid the war on terror. In the following chapter, the authors debate if such efforts increase homeland security at the cost of civil liberties.

*"What is not needed is groups of con-
gressionally empowered vigilantes
roaming the country at will looking for
'homegrown terrorism.'"*

The Violent Radicalization
and Homegrown Terrorism
Prevention Act Infringes on
Civil Liberties

Philip Giraldi

*In the following viewpoint, Philip Giraldi asserts that the Violent
Radicalization and Homegrown Terrorism Prevention Act of
2007 is among the latest in America's long tradition of civil
liberties-violating legislations targeting groups and individuals
perceived to threaten the country. The author alleges that, if enacted, the bill would give the government overriding powers to
investigate and punish alleged "homegrown terrorists." In fact,
he claims that its vague definitions of terrorism could be used to
designate various civil rights activists, peace demonstrators, and
Muslim individuals and organizations as "radicals" or "extremists." Giraldi is a former officer of the Central Intelligence Agency
and partner in Cannistraro Associates, a security consultancy.*

Philip Giraldi, "The Violent Radicalization and Homegrown Terrorism Prevention Act,"
Huffington Post, November 26, 2007. Reproduced by permission.

As you read, consider the following questions:

1. According to the author, what did the Alien and Sedition Act establish?

2. What would the Violent Radicalization and Homegrown Terrorism Prevention Act allow its commission members to do, as described by Giraldi?

3. Who would be defined as "suspects" under the bill, in Giraldi's view?

There has been a long tradition of fear-mongering legislation in the United States directed against groups and individuals believed to threaten the established order. The first such measures were the Alien and Sedition Acts passed by Congress in 1798 during the administration of the second president of the United States, John Adams. The Acts, consisting of four separate laws, made it more difficult to become a citizen, sought to control real or imagined foreign agents operating in the United States, and also gave the government broad powers to control "sedition." Sedition was defined as "resisting any law of the United States or any act of the President" punishable by a prison sentence of up to two years. It also made illegal "false, scandalous or malicious writing" directed against either the government or government officials. The next president, Thomas Jefferson, declared that three out of the four laws were unconstitutional and pardoned everyone who had been convicted under them.

Early in the last century, hysterical fear of anarchists resulted in the conviction and execution of [Fernando Nicola] Sacco and [Bartolomeo] Vanzetti in 1927 despite clear evidence that the two men were innocent. A few years later, in 1934, a Special Committee on Un-American Activities was set up by Congress to monitor the activities of fascists in the United States. Ironically, the two congressmen who were most instrumental in the establishment of the committee, Samuel Dickstein of New York and Martin Dies of Texas, both Democrats, were themselves tainted by activities that might reasonably be described as Un-American. Dickstein was himself a paid agent of the Soviet NKVD intelligence agency and Dies regularly spoke at Ku Klux Klan rallies. After the Second World War, the committee was renamed the House Un-American Activities Committee (HUAC) and focused almost exclusively on Communists, continuing to do so until it was incorporated into the House Judiciary Committee in 1974. Concurrent with HUAC on the Senate side, Joseph McCarthy of Wisconsin, a Republican, became the public face of anti-communism in the early 1950s, with his frequent claims that Communists had infiltrated the U.S. government at various levels. Few of the claims could be substantiated, however, and McCarthy eventually fell out of favor and was censured by the Senate.

A Virtual Avalanche of Legislation and Commissions

More recently, there has been the post 9/11 [September 11, 2001 terrorist attacks] creation of a virtual avalanche of legislation and commissions designed to protect the country at the expense of the Bill of Rights. The two Patriot Acts of 2001 and 2006 and the Military Commissions Act of 2006 have collectively limited constitutional rights to free speech, freedom of association, freedom from illegal search, the right to habeas corpus, prohibition of cruel and unusual punishment, and freedom from the illegal seizure of private property. The First, Fourth, Fifth, Sixth, and Eighth Amendments in the Bill of Rights have all been disregarded in the rush to make it easier to investigate people, put them in jail, and torture them if necessary. A recent executive order of July 17th, 2007, goes even farther, authorizing the president to seize the property of anyone who "Threatens Stabilization Efforts in Iraq." The government's own Justice Department decides what constitutes "threatening stabilization efforts" and the order does not permit a challenge to the information that the seizure is based on.

No Rationale for New Legislation

The U.S. Constitution, domestic criminal law, and international law already provide the government with a plethora of effective tools to investigate potential threats and protect its citizens against terrorism. The deficiencies that contributed to the failure to thwart previous acts of homegrown terrorism were not deficiencies in legal authority, but rather in the ways that the existing authority responded to intelligence information. There is no rationale, then, for Congress or the Executive to pursue unconstitutional avenues such as preventive and indefinite detention, torture and abuse, and unlawful surveillance to combat terrorism.

Center for Constitutional Rights,
"Here Come the Thought Police: The Violent Radicalization
Homegrown Terrorism Prevention Act of 2007," 2007.
http://ccrjustice.org.

One would have thought that the systematic dismantling of the Constitution of the United States would have been enough to satisfy even the most Jacobin neoconservative, but there is more on the horizon, and it is coming from people who call themselves Democrats. The mainstream media has made no effort to inform the public of the impending Violent Radicalization and Homegrown Terrorism Prevention Act. The Act, which was sponsored by Congresswoman Jane Harman of California, was passed in the House by an overwhelming 405 to 6 vote on October 24th [2007] and is now awaiting approval by the Senate Homeland Security Committee, which is headed by Senator Joseph Lieberman of Connecticut. It is believed that approval by the committee will take place shortly, to be followed by passage by the entire Senate.

Harman's bill contends that the United States will soon have to deal with homegrown terrorists and that something must be done to anticipate and neutralize the problem. The act deals with the issue through the creation of a congressional commission that will be empowered to hold hearings, conduct investigations, and designate various groups as "homegrown terrorists." The commission will be tasked to propose new legislation that will enable the government to take punitive action against both the groups and the individuals who are affiliated with them. Like Joe McCarthy and HUAC in the past, the commission will travel around the United States and hold hearings to find the terrorists and root them out. Unlike inquiries in the past where the activity was carried out collectively, the act establishing the Violent Radicalization and Homegrown Terrorism Prevention Commission will empower all the members on the commission to arrange hearings, obtain testimony, and even to administer oaths to witnesses, meaning that multiple hearings could be running simultaneously in various parts of the country. The ten commission members will be selected for their "expertise," though most will be appointed by Congress itself and will reflect the usual political interests. They will be paid for their duties at the senior executive pay scale level and will have staffs and consultants to assist them. Harman's bill does not spell out terrorist behavior and leaves it up to the Commission itself to identify what is terrorism and what isn't. Language inserted in the act does partially define "homegrown terrorism" as "planning" or "threatening" to use force to promote a political objective, meaning that just thinking about doing something could be enough to merit the terrorist label. The act also describes "violent radicalization" as the promotion of an "extremist belief system" without attempting to define "extremist."

As currently envisioned, the Commission will not operate in perpetuity. After the group has done its work, in eighteen months' time, a Center of Excellence for the Prevention of Violent Radicalization and Homegrown Terrorism will be established to study the lessons learned. The center will operate either out of the Department of Homeland Security or out of an appropriate academic institution and will be tasked with continuing to monitor the homegrown terrorism problem and proposing legislation and other measures to counter it.

Bloated and Dysfunctional

As should be clear from the vagueness of the definitions, the Violent Radicalization and Homegrown Terrorism Prevention Act could easily be abused to define any group that is pressuring the political system as "terrorist," ranging from polygamists, to second amendment rights supporters, anti-abortion protesters, anti-tax agitators, immigration activists, and peace demonstrators. In reality, of course, it will be primarily directed against Muslims and Muslim organizations. Given that, there is the question of who will select which groups will be investigated by the roving commissions. There is no evidence to suggest that there will be any transparent or objective screening process. Through their proven access both to the media and to Congress, the agenda will undoubtedly be shaped by the usual players including David Horowitz, Daniel Pipes, Steve Emerson, and Frank Gaffney who see a terrorist hiding under every rock, particularly if the rock is concealing a Muslim. They and their associates will undoubtedly find plenty of terrorists and radical groups to investigate. Many of the suspects will inevitably be "anti-American" professors at various universities and also groups of Palestinians organized against the Israeli occupation, but it will be easy to use the commission formula to sweep them all in for examination.

The view that 9/11 has "changed everything" is unfortunately all too true. It has unleashed American paranoia, institutionalized mistrust of foreigners, and created a fantasy universe in which a United States beset by enemies must do anything and everything to counter the alien threat. If it were a sane world, it would be difficult to imagine why anyone would believe that a Violent Radicalization and Homegrown Terrorism Prevention Act is even necessary. The United States has spent hundreds of billions of dollars in strengthening law enforcement and intelligence capabilities against terrorists and has every tool imaginable to investigate and make arrests. It has created a whole new bloated and dysfunctional branch of government in the Department of Homeland Security. What is not needed is groups of congressionally empowered vigilantes roaming the country at will looking for "homegrown terrorism."

| *"Radical thinking is not a crime and this legislation does not turn radical thinking into criminal behavior."*

The Violent Radicalization and Homegrown Terrorism Prevention Act Does Not Infringe on Civil Liberties

U.S. House of Representatives, Committee on Homeland Security

The Committee on Homeland Security, Majority Staff, was created by the U.S. House of Representatives in 2002 in response to the terrorist attacks of September 11, 2001. The Majority Staff argues, in the following viewpoint, that the Violent Radicalization and Homegrown Terrorism Prevention Act of 2007 is a bill intended to aid the study of domestic radicalization and terrorism and does not infringe on civil liberties. They reject allegations that, if enacted, it would regulate free speech; place Americans under government surveillance; and target specific races, ethnicities, and religions. In fact, the Majority Staff insists that

U.S. House of Representatives, Committee on Homeland Security, "Fact Sheet: Understanding H.R. 1955, The Violent Radicalization and Homegrown Terrorism Prevention Act of 2007," 2007.

prominent privacy and civil liberties groups provided consulta-tion during each phase of the bill's development to ensure civil rights are protected.

As you read, consider the following questions:

1. According to the Majority Staff, what does the Violent Radicalization and Homegrown Terrorism Prevention Act create and establish?
2. How does the Majority Staff counter the argument that the bill criminalizes political association?
3. What examples does the Majority Staff provide to support their claim that violent radicalization and terrorism is a serious domestic concern?

The bipartisan Violent Radicalization and Homegrown Terrorism Prevention Act of 2007 passed the House by a vote of 404-6. The bill received overwhelming support because it is a common sense approach to studying the unique threats of violent radicalization and homegrown terrorism in the United States. At every stage of development of the bill, feedback and guidance were sought, received, and incorporated from promi-nent privacy and civil liberties groups to ensure that the bill is consistent with the constitutional protections that we all hold dear.

The purpose of H.R. 1955 is to *study* violent radicalization and homegrown terrorism using a method that has worked in the past: the establishment of a National Commission. This approach worked prior to September 11, 2001 with the Na-tional Commission on Terrorism, which set the stage for America's counterterrorism strategy prior to the September 11 [2001] attacks. It worked again with the National Commission on Terrorists Attacks upon the United States, which in the wake of the attacks made recommendations that strengthened and solidified our current approach to fighting terrorism both domestically and abroad. This new Commission will follow their example and serve our country by providing answers to the indigenous threat of violent radicalization and home-grown terrorism.

The Commissioners will not be appointed solely by the President. Rather, the leadership of both parties, in addition to the Chairs and Ranking Members of the relevant House and Senate Committees will select individuals from a broad array of disciplines, including constitutional law. The Commission will be tasked with providing Congress with a series of reports with the Commission's findings and legislative recommenda-tions. *As with the 9/11 Commission and other national commis-sions, at the end of the day, it is Congress that decides which, if any, changes to the law, should be adopted.* The Commission will be a part of the Legislative branch and will therefore be independent of the Executive branch and its agencies.

This legislation in no way restricts thought or speech. Both of these are legal activities that should be encouraged by all segments of our society and are welcomed in our system of open debate and dialogue. Radical thinking is not a crime and this legislation does not turn radical thinking into criminal behavior.

The Truth About H.R. 1955

This legislation is a vital step toward securing America and mitigating against an American citizen engaging in a terrorist attack on American soil.

H.R. 1955 accomplishes the following:

- It creates a National Commission to examine the causes of violent radicalization and homegrown terrorism and propose concrete recommendations and legislative strat-egies for mitigating these threats.

- It establishes a Center of Excellence for the Prevention of Radicalization and Homegrown Terrorism that will study the social, criminal, political, psychological and

A Growing Trend

Today, one of the most frequently visited English language Web sites that preaches hate, violence and radicalized views of Islam is operated by a 21-year-old U.S. citizen from the comfort of his parents' home in North Carolina. Some may say these incidents are isolated cases, but I believe that they are indicative of a growing trend of homegrown terrorism in this country.

Bennie Thompson,
"The Violent Radicalization and Homegrown Terrorist Act,"
Congressional Record, *October 23, 2007. www.govtrack.us.*

economic roots of violent radicalization and home-grown terrorism and provide homeland security officials across the government with solutions to these threats.

- It requires our homeland security officials to reach out to other nations that have experienced homegrown terrorism in the past to benefit from the lessons learned by those nations.

- It protects the civil rights and civil liberties of Americans to ensure that in our effort to secure our nation from domestic threats, we abide by the rights and safeguards guaranteed by our Constitution.

Myths vs. Facts

Myth: *H.R. 1955 is a "thought crime" bill that attempts to legislate constitutionally protected speech.*

Fact: H.R. 1955 does *not* legislate thought or protected political expression and free speech. There are no provisions seeking to change the criminal code or set up a "Big Brother" regime to put Americans under surveillance.

Myth: *H.R. 1955 criminalizes constitutionally protected behavior such as political association.*

Fact: H.R. 1955 does *not* criminalize behavior. The bill does not create any new crimes, criminal penalties, nor does it encourage the Commission to do so. On the contrary, H.R. 1955 requires the Department of Homeland Security, through its Privacy Office and Office of Civil Rights and Civil Liberties, to create an auditing mechanism to ensure that any policy stemming from the actions of the Commission will not violate anyone's rights. The results of this audit will be included in the Commission's annual report to Congress.

Myth: *H.R. 1955 discriminates against particular races, ethnicities and religions.*

Fact: H.R. 1955 does *not* alienate any particular race, ethnicity or religious group. To the contrary, the bill includes a provision that states that "individuals prone to violent radicalization, homegrown terrorism, and ideologically based violence span all races, ethnicities, and religious beliefs, and individuals should not be targeted based solely on race, ethnicity, or religion."

Myth: *H.R. 1955 will lead to Internet censorship.*

Fact: H.R. 1955 neither targets the Internet nor seeks to censor its usage. The Internet is a robust communications tool that can be used to educate, inspire, challenge, entertain, and stimulate intellectual curiosity and promote awareness and understanding across cultures and national borders. The protection of the Internet from government interference is in our national interest.

Myth: *H.R. 1955 is unnecessary because the threat of violent radicalization and homegrown terrorism does not exist in the United States.*

Fact: While it is true that European countries have experienced violent radicalization and homegrown terrorism at a greater proportion than the United States, we are not immune. The arrests of U.S. citizens who were plotting attacks against the Fort Dix military base in New Jersey and JFK airport in New York earlier this year [2007] remind us that the threat in this country is real. And we must never forget that the most deadly act of terrorism perpetrated on American soil prior to September 11, 2001 was committed by American citizen Timothy McVeigh, who was responsible for the death of over 180 people, including small children, in one day. These examples indicate that we need to be ahead of the curve. H.R. 1955 instructs our Government to reach out to other Nations to learn about how they have addressed violent radicalization and homegrown terrorism in their countries. And once again, it protects the liberties of Americans by requiring our Government to evaluate what other countries have done within our own Constitutional framework and system of safeguards and protections.

"There is nothing intrinsically wrong with profiling. Some people, quite simply, pose greater security risks than others."

Ethnic and Religious Profiling Is Necessary

Carl F. Horowitz

Carl F. Horowitz is the director of the Organized Labor Accountability Project of the National Legal and Policy Center in Fall Church, Virginia. In the following viewpoint, Horowitz asserts that racial and religious profiling is a necessary defense against terrorism in a post-September 11, 2001, world. Horowitz argues that Muslim extremists commit the vast majority of terrorist acts against the United States in subterfuge, so their movements and activities in the country must be scrutinized. Increased surveillance of suspicious Muslims—which was enabled through the Patriot Act—have stifled terrorist activity and prevented potential attacks without violating civil liberties, he claims.

As you read, consider the following questions:

1. As stated by Horowitz, what has eroded national identity and security?

Carl F. Horowitz, "Profiling in an Age of Terrorism," *Social Contract*, vol. 17, Fall 2006, pp. 47–51. Reproduced by permission.

2. How does Horowitz use the example of Muhammad al-Qahtani to support his argument for profiling Muslims in the United States?

3. How does the author describe "fourth-generation warfare"?

Good evening. I'd like to thank the Robert A. Taft Club for giving me the opportunity to speak on an incendiary subject: ethnic and religious profiling as an anti-terrorism strategy. Some people, on the Right as well as the Left, believe that examining movement into and within the U.S. by Muslims, especially Arab Muslims, is irreconcilable with preserving basic civil liberties. With all due respect, I happen to reject that view. There is no reason to believe that a policy of vetting individuals who belong to the ethno-religious entity responsible for most of the terrorism against this country harms law-abiding citizens. Toward that end, I offer a defense of ethnic and religious profiling, and one of its primary tools, the USA Patriot Act.

Profiling: Workable and Necessary

National identity and security now more than ever go together. The terror attacks against the World Trade Center and the Pentagon [in 2001] were the result of decades of erosion of our national identity and national security. They were the result of a comfortable self-delusion that all ethnic, national and religious groups want to be, and are equally capable of being, Americanized. It's as if entry into this country is an act of de facto patriotism. The reality, of course, is that many people come to this country with every intention of conquering us, or at any rate, flouting our laws. More invaders than immigrants, such people live in a state of infantile wish-fulfillment that equates mass murder and religious obligation. And they have a rather nasty tendency to be Muslims, especially from the Middle East.

Now unlike certain misguided "patriots," I regard as poisonous the psychology of Battered American Syndrome. This is the famous we-got-what-was-coming-to-us argument. The 9/11 [September 11, 2001] terror attacks, we are told incessantly, constituted "blowback," just desserts for our gratuitous meddling in the Middle East. This is anti-Americanism, whether it comes from the Right or the Left. It certainly is inadequate to the task of understanding the nature of our terrorist enemies.

It is true that most Muslims living in this country, not to mention those who plan to come, are not terrorists by any stretch. But a good many are the kind who would give terrorists aid, comfort and applause. And as we all know now, it only takes a few dozen terrorists to inflict nationwide mayhem. Back when our immigration policy really functioned—that is to say, prior to the 1965 amendments to the Immigration and Nationality Act—*virtually none of these people, even the sympathizers, would have gotten into the U.S.*

That leads to a governing principle. To stand an old expression on its head, the best offense is a good defense. About 175 years ago [military strategist] Carl von Clausewitz put it this way:

> Defense is simply the stronger form of war, the one that makes the enemy's defeat more certain . . . We maintain unequivocally that the form of warfare we call defense not only offers greater probability of victory than attack, but that its victories can attain the same proportions and results.

Profiling Based on a Statistical Fact

In today's context, on a practical level, that means that the movement, conversations and other behavior of Muslims, whether native-born or foreign-born, need to be scrutinized, monitored and analyzed—in a word, profiled. In all likelihood, they are not radical anti-Americans. Yet on the other hand, they just might be. And unlike mere dissenters, these

221

people are at war with us. *That* is the underlying reality of the cliche, "the post-9/11 environment." It is a statistical fact: A young Muslim man is tens of thousands of times more likely than anyone else in the world to commit an act of terrorism. He *should* be profiled.

Consider the following scenario: I am an airport security inspector. A young Middle Eastern man or women walks up to my checkpoint. Would I be inclined to ask (or have another person ask) this passenger some extra questions about his background and beliefs before I let him through? You bet I would. Equally to the point, I'm *not* going to give extra attention to persons who don't look Middle Eastern or display outward signs of Islamic belief. To ask extra questions of each and every passenger, on a practical basis, would be a logistical disaster. Taking such inconvenience to its extreme, almost nobody would choose to fly.

There is nothing intrinsically wrong with profiling. Some people, quite simply, pose greater security risks than others. Membership in a particular ethnic or religious group is a valid marker for assuming and judging unobserved behavioral traits in another person, especially when we have no other information to go on at that moment in time. To insist otherwise is to not live in the real world.

Can profiling produce results? Purer-than-thou libertarians insist the U.S. government is incapable of defending us from terrorists. I say baloney. When federal law enforcement is allowed to do what local cops long have been able to do—monitor, question and detain criminal suspects based on observable physical traits—they can catch terrorists planning their misdeeds. And they *have* caught them, despite pressure from supervisors to look the other way. . . .

In August 2001, a month before the 9/11 attacks, a certain Muhammad al-Qahtani, a Saudi, was turned away from this country while attempting to enter the U.S. at Orlando International Airport. Customs officer Jose Melendez-Perez understood the real requirements of his job rather than the bureaucratically mandated requirements. Though he'd been warned by his superiors against racial profiling of Arabs, he responded, "I don't care. This guy's a bad guy. I can see it in his eyes." Officer Melendez-Perez was right. There *was* something in this guy's eyes.

As al-Qahtani was being led off, he turned around and announced, "I'll be back." He kept his word, though under unplanned circumstances. Qahtani was identified as the would-be 20th hijacker. In the recent trial of Zacarias Moussaoui, it had come out that 9/11 mastermind Khalid Shaikh Muhammad had pointed to al-Qahtani as the hijacker who would "complete the group." His assignment: United Flight 93, the one that crashed in rural Pennsylvania, now the subject of a splendid new movie, a suicide hijacking mission whose intended target, based on all available evidence, was either the White House or the U.S. Capitol. The three other planes each had five hijackers; Flight 93 had only four. That fact might have been why the latter's passengers were able to overpower the terrorists. Our armed forces in Afghanistan, by the way, managed to track Qahtani down. He's now reportedly a resident of Guantanamo Bay prison. . . .

Yet the [George W.] Bush administration has learned little. Federal officials, if anything, appear more frightened of offending the sensibilities of Islamic and Arab "civil-rights" groups than going the extra mile to track down and arrest the most dangerous criminals in the world. On June 17, 2003, acting on the stern advice of President Bush, the Department of Justice [DOJ] ordered a total ban on racial and ethnic profiling at dozens of federal agencies. The DOJ guidelines directly affected around 120,000 law enforcement officers at the FBI, the DEA [Drug Enforcement Agency], the Department of Homeland Security, ATF [Bureau of Alcohol, Tobacco, Firearms, and Explosives], the Coast Guard and elsewhere. . . .

Criminal vs. Terrorist Profiling

Indisputably, the potential benefit of a criminal profile, while certainly not trivial, extends at most to saving a small number of lives. That pales in comparison with the potential benefit of a terrorist profile—a matter of saving thousands or conceivably hundreds of thousands of lives. On those grounds alone, it seems rational to protest the former while applauding the latter.

Robert A. Levy,
"Blacks for Profiling: Criminal vs. Terrorist Profiling,"
National Review, *February 6, 2002.*
www.nationalreview.com.

The Patriot Act Reconsidered

The case for profiling, put simply, is far stronger than the case against it. Whether the USA Patriot Act is an appropriate vehicle for profiling is a separate issue. Let us go into a bit of detail. This legislation, officially known as the Uniting and Strengthening America by Providing Appropriate Tools Required to Intercept and Obstruct Terrorism Act, does not formally authorize profiling persons on ethnic, racial or religious grounds. Yet given its overwhelming passage in the House and the Senate in October 2001, only weeks after the 9/11 atrocities, the context was the danger posed by this country's current and future Islamic population. By giving law enforcement extra tools of surveillance, infiltration and arrest, and by breaking down the traditional information-sharing firewall between enforcement and intelligence agencies, the Patriot Act was meant to root out Muslim terrorists *before* they attack. Congress, after a lengthy and contentious debate, reauthorized the act in March 2006.

The law is needed, quite simply, because the enemy gives us no choice. Their mode of operation, to use military strategist William Lind's term, is "fourth-generation warfare." In this form of combat, subterfuge is everything. The Islamic terrorist radicals are masters of deception as well as destruction. Consider that:

- They don't have a national capital and, with the exception of the Chechen thugs, are in no sense nationalists.

- They don't have tanks, uniforms, infantry or battle formations.

- They don't seek summit meetings or peace talks, since they don't want to be found.

- They frequently change their laptop computers and cell phones to minimize detection of messages they send to each other.

- They use fake IDs, not exactly impossible to come by these days.

- They heavily recruit inside mosques, which our government apparently deems off-limits for infiltration.

These people live, breathe and think war 24 hours a day. And as long as they are outnumbered and outgunned, at least here in the United States, they will plan terrorist acts with the utmost of guile. That is why we must use every available tool of infiltration, including the roving wiretaps authorized by the Patriot Act. Without those wiretaps, it would be far more difficult, absent random luck, to gather evidence of a pending attack.

But hasn't the Act severely diminished our civil liberties? Critics who make this point, from [journalist] Alexander Cockburn (Left) to [libertarian] James Bovard (Right), typically denounce the law in terms of what it *would* do or *might* do. You'll notice, interestingly, that their broadsides aren't in the past tense—as in "has done." That's because there's no hard evidence—even anecdotal, much less systematic—that our liberties have been violated. A couple years ago Sen. Dianne Feinstein (D-CA) responded to a request by the ACLU [American Civil Liberties Union] to monitor the use of the Patriot Act. Her response: "We've scrubbed the area, and I have no reported abuses."

This finding should not come as a surprise. The law was written to set a very high bar of proof for a judge to issue a search warrant, wiretap authorization, or some other surveillance tool. It also authorized the creation of a civil liberties board, overseen by Congress, to ensure compliance with existing laws that protect innocent citizens. Here's what the law *has done*. It has brought terrorism-related charges against at least 400 people, many of whom are in this country illegally; more than half those charges have led to convictions. It has broken up confirmed terror cells in New York, Oregon, Virginia, and Florida. Through its information-sharing features, for example, it has led to the arrest of a Kashmir-born Islamic fundamentalist (and naturalized U.S. citizen) from Columbus, Ohio, Iyman Faris, who had been supplying al-Qaeda with information on how to blow up New York City's Brooklyn Bridge.

Terrorists continue to strike—very recently in Israel and Egypt, and [summer 2005] in London, murdering dozens of innocent people. But they haven't done anything in America since the 9/11 attacks and the anthrax letter attacks (also likely the work of Islamic extremists) in their immediate wake. It strains the imagination to suggest the Patriot Act has had nothing to do with the lack of attacks on our soil since 2001. If the Committee on American Islamic Relations, the ACLU and convicted lawyer Lynne Stewart are enraged over the law's "insensitivity" toward Muslims, that should be of no concern to anyone with patriotic instincts.

Conclusion: The Necessity of Scrutiny

To sum up, there are two separate issues at hand: First, should profiling be used to prevent terrorism? Second, should the USA Patriot Act serve as a means of prevention? The answer in both cases is "yes." As for the first consideration, there are inherent legal and political risks in profiling. No matter how good the information, every cop runs the risk of questioning, frisking, or arresting the wrong person. As for the second, while the Patriot Act may require amending, that's a far cry from repeal.

The Patriot Act has shown it is capable of protecting us from Islamic terrorists, without violating basic liberties. It is mild stuff, really. Unlike during World War II, for example, we don't have rationing, rent control, endless war bond appeals, film and newspaper censorship, draft registration, and other intrusive demands by the State for collective sacrifice. This is all to the good. But until Muslims, the world over, cease in any way to take part in, or endorse, the mass murder of Americans, I shall willingly put up with the Patriot Act's rather negligible excesses.

The long-range goal of America—and the rest of the West—should be defusing Islamic aggression. Since this isn't about to happen anytime soon, we should focus on self-defense. The necessity of deploying troops in the Middle East, and risking more of our men coming home in body bags, is open to debate. The necessity of scrutinizing people who share ethnic and religious traits of our avowed enemies should not be.

In the end, America is our country to defend. And this Northern paleoconservative is willing to defend it. Thank you very much.

| "The war on terrorism has lent profiling
the veneer of legitimacy...."

Ethnic and Religious Profiling Violates Civil Liberties

Chisun Lee

In the following viewpoint, Chisun Lee contends that ethnic and religious profiling in the wake of the September 11, 2001, terrorist attacks has rolled back civil rights. Lee insists that terrorist profiling of Muslims is the same as discriminatory profiling of African Americans and Latinos. Lee contends that thousands of innocent Arab, Muslim, and South Asian immigrants have been disproportionately rounded up and jailed for minor infractions without resulting in any terrorist charges. Ultimately, the author warns that such government bias and intrusion opens the door to sweeping discrimination against individuals belonging to these groups. Lee is a contributing writer to the Village Voice.

As you read, consider the following questions:

1. Why does the author insist that a major civil rights victory nearly occurred in 2000?

2. What "technical infractions" were immigrants profiled for terrorism jailed for, in Lee's view?

3. According to Lee, what is the state of profiling for African Americans and Latinos?

Four years ago [2000] the nation stood at the cusp of a major civil rights victory. Activists from across the country rallied in Washington, D.C., to end racial profiling. Polls showed a majority of Americans opposed the practice. Al Gore vowed that as president he would make a law banning it, "the first civil rights act of the 21st century."

George W. Bush agreed with his opponent. "I can't imagine what it would be like to be singled out because of race and stopped and harassed," he said during one 2000 debate. "That's just flat wrong." Then he did Gore one better: "There is other forms of racial profiling that goes on in America. Arab Americans are racially profiled. . . . People are stopped, and we got to do something about that."

But today his administration's reaction to the 2001 terrorist attacks has not only betrayed Bush's own rhetoric, but worse, it has undermined the political force of the anti-profiling movement in general—the force that made it a profound civil rights cause, not just a policy debate. By couching group-based profiling as necessary to homeland security, the government has traded the principles of universal equality and individual dignity for the presumption of safety. Nearly no one this election year [2004] has been bold enough to hint at the outrage that once powered a bipartisan movement. It has become impossible to be righteous about racial profiling without encountering the inevitable "But what about 9–11?"

What about it? Three years out, the question demands more than a knee-jerk nod. A thoughtful look will show that the terrorist attacks did not make such profiling any less wrong than it was on September 10, 2001. In fact, it is all the more insidious today, because the war on terrorism has lent profiling the veneer of legitimacy—even urgency, after alerts such as the one regarding financial centers last weekend [July 2004].

As this modern civil rights movement begins to put itself back together, with a renewed push for federal legislation, it is important to realize that racial profiling has not gotten any less wrong—the government is just more willing to do the wrong thing. And to be willing to do the wrong thing is a devastating rejection of the values of American life.

One and the Same

"Racial profiling is being stopped driving while black or driving while Hispanic. This is not racial profiling," said Mark Corallo, spokesperson for the Department of Justice, when asked about the administration's 9–11-related operations. He voiced precisely the kind of thinking that has obscured the crisis of profiling for the past three years.

Trawling for terrorists and pulling over motorists in search of drugs are in fact the same thing. While it may be acceptable to target people based on a racial or ethnic description if—and only if—there is some specific indication that those particular people are actually criminals, broad sweeps based on general traits are never OK. Not only are they unlikely to yield "hits" and certain to humiliate innocent parties, but such dragnets also violate this nation's fundamental principle that people will be treated as individuals and not according to stereotypes.

"You either have racial profiling, or you don't have racial profiling. You can't have it both ways," says LaShawn Warren, a leader in pushing for passage of the End Racial Profiling Act of 2004, currently a bill with support from 124 members of the House and 16 of the Senate. As a national legislative counsel for the American Civil Liberties Union, she has been struggling to show Congress members that FBI questioning and immigration roundups of people who appear to be Arab or Muslim—whatever that looks like—are "no different than the old kind of racial profiling that we said was wrong."

There is little wonder that some people refuse to believe her. The Bush administration has led the way. In his long-promised racial profiling ban, announced with great fanfare in June 2003, Bush told federal law-enforcement agencies that "racial profiling is wrong and will not be tolerated" and that "stereotyping certain races as having a greater propensity to commit crimes is absolutely prohibited." (The directive, which is not a law, lacks any enforcement mechanism, so the prohibition is absolute only in theory.) But he created a crippling exception: "The above standards do not affect current federal policy with respect to law enforcement activities and other efforts to defend and safeguard against threats to national security."

In effect, that "national security" loophole has become the exception that would erase the rule. Like a political ray gun, it neutralizes any critic who would cry racism or xenophobia [fear of foreigners] when it comes to 9–11-related profiling.

Corallo pointed out, "There were 19 hijackers who were from an Islamic background." Certainly it makes sense to hunt for people like them—but like them how? There was once a time when people defended the "driving while black" variety of profiling, because searching certain minorities for drugs was said to make sense. But as public indignation mounted over the years, the U.S. Customs Service, for example, scaled back its profiling and turned to behavior- and intelligence-based investigations instead. Drug-runner apprehensions more than doubled.

This administration has not scored big points for its investigative depth. Nevertheless, it "outright rejects" allegations that it engages in broad, stereotype-based profiling, Corallo said. "I understand what they're saying when they feel there's a focus on them," he said of Arab, Muslim, and South Asian immigrants and citizens who complain of biased treatment, "but there's not."

Maybe it depends on how one defines "focus."

Pervasive Pattern

Tens of thousands of people from Muslim, Arab, and South Asian backgrounds have been targeted by the government in a slew of sweeps since 9–11. Teenage boys and men from 25 predominantly Muslim countries, none accused of any crime, at one point were ordered to report to immigration offices for questioning and fingerprinting, or risk arrest and deportation. By the end of the "special registration," over 82,000 individuals had complied and over 13,000 were slated for deportation as a result.

The FBI initiated two official rounds of interviews it called "voluntary" with some 8,000 immigrants and citizens of Arab, Muslim, and South Asian backgrounds. Community advocates claim that agents show up unannounced all the time—although Corallo said, "People are not getting knocks on the door and questioned." In everyday encounters with local police, co-workers, and neighbors, thousands more have been reported to authorities and detained, according to these advocacy groups. The Justice Department's own internal watchdog revealed in 2003 that scores of immigrants experienced physical abuse or due process violations while in government custody.

No matter that exactly zero terrorism-related charges have emerged from these initiatives, and that all the high-profile cases have resulted from real investigative work or pure accident. (From Timothy McVeigh to John Walker Lindh, the most infamous national security threats do not fit the Arab terrorist profile at all.) The roundups continue, according to weekly e-mail updates among immigration lawyers and advocates.

Well, these are immigrants, one argument goes. They're not supposed to be here in the first place, and they don't enjoy the same rights as citizens. Corallo claims that border control has "stopped 12 known terrorists from getting into the country. We also caught hundreds of convicted felons." (The

RELAX... YOU CAN PICK 'EM UP AFTER THE WAR!

CIVIL LIBERTIES

Voice could find no mention of these figures, outside of Corallo's comment.) The vast majority jailed as a result of the immigration crackdowns are, in fact, guilty of something—although almost universally of technical infractions like staying past a visa deadline or not taking enough class credits to fulfill the student-visitor requirements. Putting aside the important debate about whether prolonged detention is the right response to a paperwork problem, these folks technically are subject to monitoring by the U.S. government.

Yet this monitoring has hardly been equally applied. "They weren't calling in immigrants from Great Britain," the ACLU's Warren points out. "There's a really unjustifiable distinction being made."

That distinction is where 9–11-related profiling and the more traditional notion of racial profiling meet. That distinction is stereotype. Whether based on race, religion, or national origin, the special burden of a profiled person is being plagued by negative assumptions tagged to his or her "type."

233

The result of such profiling is not just indignation but rank inequality. Says Leti Volpp, author of a widely cited 2002 law article entitled "The Citizen and the Terrorist," "Being a citizen means enjoying all the rights of a citizen. But 'driving while black' was a sign that African Americans could only enjoy second-class citizen-ship." She explains that people who are perceived to be Arab or Muslim face the same injustice. Instead of the right to be considered innocent until proven guilty, for instance, they "have to prove themselves innocent."

Just last week [July 2004] it emerged that the Census Bureau had given detailed location and national-origin data on Arab Americans—U.S. citizens—to the Department of Homeland Security [DHS]. DHS claimed it wanted the information in order to post Arabic language signs in the right airports. But as the news shot around civil rights listservs, people recalled how census data was used during World War II to identify Japanese Americans who would be sent to U.S. internment camps.

Though the administration may deny it, former federal appellate judge Timothy Lewis, who was appointed to the Third Circuit by the first President George Bush, insists that there has been a widespread pattern of unjustified profiling by the government since 9–11. He agreed to chair a series of national public hearings on "war on drugs" and "war on terror" profiling last year for Amnesty International USA, only after the organization agreed to invite law enforcement representatives for fairness's sake.

"What struck me more than anything was the pervasiveness of the practice," said Lewis, who was also once a federal prosecutor and is now of counsel at Schnader Harrison Segal & Lewis in Washington, D.C. "I'm talking about going after people without any criminal predicate. Racial profiling is a national phenomenon. And the hearings barely scratched the surface."

The profiling of blacks and Latinos continues to thrive, even as the once robust opposition to it has deflated "in the frenzied atmosphere after 9–11," as Lewis put it. From Massachusetts to Missouri to Texas, studies as recent as this May [2004] showed that minorities were still disproportionately—in one state as much as 40 percent more often—subjected to traffic stops, at rates unjustified by their actual record of possessing drugs. In one egregious situation, police in Charlottesville, Virginia, indiscriminately demanded DNA samples from area black men in their hunt for a serial rapist. The dragnet continued for over two years before public scrutiny this spring finally convinced authorities to stop.

Private Hate, Public Problem

For 9–11-related-profiling victims, the element of "foreignness" gives discrimination a special twist, says Volpp. "People who look a certain way are assumed not to be citizens to begin with," but rather unwelcome outsiders, she says. That perception makes them especially vulnerable, not just to government intrusions but to private acts of violence.

Over a thousand 9–11-related bias incidents, including harassment and physical attacks, have been recorded since 2001 by groups such as the Council on American-Islamic Relations and the Sikh Coalition, and by the Justice Department's Civil Rights Division. They have included assaults, arson, and even killings. And those are just the incidents that have been reported by people confident or informed enough to seek out these resources.

Official profiling and private bias are connected, says Muneer Ahmad, an associate professor at American University Law School. Although no one can legislate away personal prejudices, he says, "The government sends signals and cues all the time as to what is permissible. The end of racially discriminatory laws against African Americans didn't translate instantly into substantive equality. But when the government said segregation was okay, it was communicating a lot about what was appropriate. It's one thing for racial prejudice to be a part of society, but you provide people license to engage in that kind of behavior if you don't have a policy that condemns it."

The federal government has vigorously prosecuted some hate crimes, for example one in which a Sikh postal carrier in California was shot in the neck with a pellet rifle. And President Bush has repeatedly admonished the nation not to engage in bias against Muslims and Arabs.

But Ahmad says those statements must be juxtaposed with the official profiling of people from certain backgrounds. "Condemning the private violence gives the administration political cover. If you morally condemn something, you elevate yourself."

Racial profiling can only be eradicated by a renewed social movement that exposes and opposes it. Politicians can't be trusted to buck 9–11 politics and challenge the practice on their own, without strong popular support, since they fear being labeled soft on terror. And profiling victims have almost never found justice in the courts, since judges are notoriously reluctant to apply the Constitution's equal treatment mandate in a way that might interfere with police discretion.

Indeed, President Bush was oddly prescient when he said in 2000, "Racial profiling isn't just an issue with local police forces. It's an issue throughout our society. And as we become a diverse society, we're going to have to deal with it more and more."

He couldn't have known how much more urgent that message would become after four years of his leadership. But at this moment when reasonable fears of terrorism too often find expression in unreasonable fears of certain people, and the government flatly denies that it is part of the prejudice problem, only a broad social movement can achieve the civil rights victory that seemed so possible four years ago. The effort to end racial profiling is part of the ongoing struggle to make the American dream of equality and dignity come true for everyone.

Periodical Bibliography

The following articles have been selected to supplement the diverse views presented in this chapter.

Stanley C. Brubaker   "The Misunderstood Fourth Amendment," *Weekly Standard*, March 6, 2006.

Erwin Chemerinsky   "Civil Liberties and the War on Terrorism," *Washburn Law Journal*, January 7, 2006.

David Cole   "How Not to Fight Terrorism," *Washington Post*, May 5, 2006.

The Economist   "Is Torture Ever Justified? Terrorism and Civil Liberty," September 22, 2007.

Anthony Giddens   "'Scaring People May Be the Only Way to Avoid the Risks of New-Style Terrorism,'" *New Statesman*, January 10, 2005.

Laura Goering   "'Big Brother' Bothers Britain," *Chicago Tribune*, October 27, 2008.

Liz Halloran   "Everyone's Spinning the Spying," *U.S. News & World Report*, February 5, 2006.

Eric Lichtblau   "New Guidelines Would Give FBI Broader Powers," *New York Times*, August 20, 2008.

Michelle Malkjn   "Racial Profiling: A Matter of Survival," *USA Today*, August 16, 2004.

Walter Williams   "Airport Security and Racial Profiling," *Capitalism Magazine*, December 20, 2006.

Matthew Yglesias   "Profiles Encouraged," *American Prospect*, August 2, 2005.

Kim Zetter   "Why Racial Profiling Doesn't Work," *Salon*, August 22, 2005.

For Further Discussion

Chapter 1

1. Do you agree with Steven J. Heyman that free speech is limited by other civil rights? Use examples from the viewpoints to develop your answer.

2. Liam Martin insists that hate speech has little social value. Conversely, Jonathan Gallagher maintains that what is considered "hate speech" can be valuable to debate. In your opinion, who makes the more compelling argument? Explain your answer.

3. Do you agree with Sandy Starr's assertion that the Internet exaggerates the prevalence and legitimacy of extremist and fanatical beliefs? Why or why not?

Chapter 2

1. Americans United for Separation of Church and State claims that the wall of separation between church and state contributes to religious harmony. In contrast, Daniel L. Dreisbach states that intolerant groups appropriate the wall metaphor to keep religious beliefs out of politics. Do Americans United's arguments for the separation of church and state promote religious intolerance? Use examples from the viewpoints to develop your answer.

2. George W. Bush suggests that lessening the restrictions for faith-based charitable organizations to receive federal funds recognizes their objectives, not their beliefs. Nonetheless, Richard B. Katskee argues that lessening these restrictions diverts funds from experienced faith-based charitable organizations that do not favor their followers. In your opinion, should faith-based organizations receive more federal funds? Why or why not?

3. Antonin Scalia claims that religious displays other than
   the Ten Commandments have endured on public and government property and have not been prohibited or
   deemed unconstitutional. In your opinion, is Scalia's claim
   a persuasive argument for the public display of the Ten
   Commandments? Explain your answer.

Chapter 3

1. David H. Holtzman contends that technology has placed
   privacy in jeopardy, while Michael Turner insists that
   technology should not be blamed for all threats to privacy
   and shifts some responsibility to its users. In your opinion, does Holtzman unfairly blame technology for privacy
   threats? Why or why not?

2. John Edwards claims that people are willing to sacrifice
   some privacy in exchange for security. Do you agree or
   disagree with the author? Use examples from the viewpoints to develop your answer.

Chapter 4

1. Philip Giraldi insists that the vague language of the Violent Radicalization and Homegrown Terrorism Prevention
   Act of 2007 can be used to designate civil rights activists,
   peace demonstrators, and Muslims. In your opinion, does
   the Majority Staff, Committee on Homeland Security, describe the act using vague language? Use examples from
   the viewpoints to develop your answer.

2. Chisun Lee argues that not all terrorists fit the Muslim
   profile. Carl F. Horowitz's profile of terrorists is predominantly Muslim. In your opinion, is Horowitz's argument
   to profile Muslims to combat terrorism justified? Explain
   your answer.

Organizations to Contact

The editors have compiled the following list of organizations concerned with the issues debated in this book. The descriptions are derived from materials provided by the organizations. All have publications or information available for interested readers. The list was compiled on the date of publication of the present volume; the information provided here may change. Be aware that many organizations take several weeks or longer to respond to inquiries, so allow as much time as possible.

American Civil Liberties Union (ACLU)
125 Broad Street, 18th Floor, New York, NY   10004
Web site: www.aclu.org

Founded in 1920, the American Civil Liberties Union (ACLU) is a nonprofit and nonpartisan organization that focuses on basic freedoms. It has more than five hundred thousand members and supporters and handles nearly six thousand court cases annually from its offices in almost every state. The ACLU publishes various materials on civil liberties, as well as a set of handbooks on individual rights.

Americans United for Separation of Church and State (AUSCS)
516 C Street NE, Washington, DC   20002
(202) 466-3234 • Fax: (202) 466-2587
E-mail: americansunited@au.org
Web site: www.au.org

Americans United for Separation of Church and State (AUSCS) works to protect religious freedom for all Americans. Its principal means of action are litigation, education, and advocacy. It opposes the passing of either federal or state laws that threaten the separation of church and state. Its publications include brochures, pamphlets, and the monthly newsletter *Church and State*.

Electronic Frontier Foundation (EFF)

454 Shotwell Street, San Francisco, CA   94110-1914
(415) 436 9333 • Fax: (415) 436 9993
E-mail: eff@eff.org
Web site: www.eff.org

The Electronic Frontier Foundation (EFF) is an organization of students and other individuals that aims to promote a better understanding of telecommunications issues. It fosters awareness of civil liberties issues arising from advancements in computer-based communications media and supports litigation to preserve, protect, and extend First Amendment rights in computing and telecommunications technologies. EFF's publications include *Building the Open Road, Crime and Puzzlement,* the quarterly newsletter *Networks & Policy,* the bi-weekly electronic newsletter *EFFector Online,* and online bulletins and publications.

Electronic Privacy Information Center (EPIC)

EPIC National Office, Washington, DC   20009
(202) 483-1140 • Fax: (202) 483-1248
Web site: http://epic.org

The Electronic Privacy Information Center (EPIC) is a public interest research center in Washington, D.C. It was established in 1994 to focus public attention on emerging civil liberties issues and to protect privacy, the First Amendment, and constitutional values. EPIC publishes an e-mail and online newsletter on civil liberties in the information age—*EPIC Alert.* It also publishes reports and books about privacy, open government, free speech, and other important topics related to civil liberties.

Free Speech Coalition (FSC)

Main Office, Canoga Park, CA   91309
(866) 372-9373 • Fax: (818) 348-9373
Web site: www.freespeechcoalition.com

Founded in 1991, the Free Speech Coalition (FSC) is a trade association for the adult entertainment industry of the United States. Its Web site offers news and legal information on censorship and free speech, as well as reports.

The Heritage Foundation
214 Massachusetts Avenue NE, Washington, DC   20002-4999
(202) 546-4400 • Fax: (202) 546-8328
E-mail: pubs@heritage.org
Web site: www.heritage.org

The Heritage Foundation is a conservative public policy organization dedicated to free-market principles, individual liberty, and limited government. It favors limiting freedom of the press when that freedom threatens national security. Its resident scholars publish position papers on a wide range of issues through publications such as the *Backgrounder* and the *First Principles* series.

Human Rights Watch (HRW)
350 Fifth Avenue, New York, NY   10118-3299
(212) 290-4700 • Fax: (212) 736-1300
E-mail: hrwnyc@hrw.org
Web site: www.hrw.org

Human Rights Watch (HRW) regularly investigates human rights abuses in over seventy countries around the world. It promotes civil liberties and defends freedom of thought, due process, and equal protection of the law. Its goal is to hold governments accountable for human rights violations they may commit against individuals because of their political, ethnic, or religious affiliations. It publishes extensive reports on human rights issues across the world, the annual *Human Rights Watch World Report*, and a publications catalog.

**National Association for the Advancement
of Colored People (NAACP)**
4805 Mt. Hope Drive, Baltimore, MD   21215
(877) NAACP-98 (622-2798)

Web site: www.naacp.org

Founded in 1909, the National Association for the Advancement of Colored People (NAACP) is a civil rights organization that works to ensure the political, educational, social, and economic equality of rights of all persons and to eliminate racial hatred and racial discrimination. It publishes a newsletter, *NAACP Advocate*, and various reports and operates a legal department and a program advocating civic engagement.

National Coalition Against Censorship (NCAC)
275 Seventh Avenue, New York, NY   10001
(212) 807-6222 • Fax: (212) 807-6245
E-mail: ncac@ncac.org
Web site: www.ncac.org

The National Coalition Against Censorship (NCAC) is an alliance of organizations committed to defending freedom of thought, inquiry, and expression by engaging in public education and advocacy on national and local levels. It publishes periodic reports and the quarterly *Censorship News*.

National Coalition for the Protection of Children and Families (NCPCF)
800 Compton Road, Cincinnati, OH   45231
(513) 521-6227
Web site: www.nationalcoalition.org

The National Coalition for the Protection of Children and Families (NCPCF) is an organization of business, religious, and civic leaders who work to defend against pornography as well as sexuality in the media. Its Web site offers brochures and other materials on protecting families against online pornography and sexual solicitation.

People for the American Way Foundation (PFAW)
2000 M Street NW, Washington, DC   20036
(202) 467-4999
Web site: www.pfaw.org

People for the American Way Foundation (PFAW) works to increase tolerance and respect for America's diverse cultures, religions, and values. It distributes educational materials, leaflets, and brochures, including the reports *Anti-Gay Politics and the Religious Right*, *The Long Shadow of Jim Crow: Voter Suppression in America*, and *Parental Rights: The Trojan Horse of the Religious Right Attack on Public Education*.

Religion in Public Education Resource Center (RPERC)
239 Trinity Hall, Chico, CA   95929-0740
(530) 898-4739
E-mail: bgrelle@csuchico.edu
Web site: www.csuchico.edu/rs/rperc/

The Religion in Public Education Resource Center (RPERC) believes religion should be studied in public schools in ways that do not promote the values or beliefs of one religion over another but that expose students to such beliefs and promote historical and cultural literacy. Its publications include *Religion and the Public Schools* and *Spotlight on Teaching About Religion in the Schools*.

Bibliography of Books

Bruce Barry   *Speechless: The Erosion of Free
                     Expression in the American Workplace.*
                     San Francisco, CA: Berrett-Koehler
                     Publishers, 2007.

Collin J. Bennett   *The Privacy Advocates: Resisting the
                     Spread of Surveillance.* Cambridge,
                     MA: MIT Press, 2008.

Amy E. Black,   *Of Little Faith: The Politics of George
Douglas L.   W. Bush's Faith-Based Initiatives.*
Koopman, and   Washington, DC: Georgetown
David K. Ryden   University Press, 2004.

Alejandro del   *Racial Profiling in America.* Upper
Carmen   Saddle River, NJ: Pearson Prentice
                     Hall, 2008.

Richard Delgado   *Understanding Words That Wound.*
and Jean Stefanic   Boulder, CO: Westview Press, 2004.

Whitfield Diffie   *Privacy on the Line: The Politics of
and Susan   Wiretapping and Encryption.* 2nd ed.
Landau   Cambridge, MA: MIT Press, 2007.

David Domke   *The God Strategy: How Religion
and Kevin Coe   Became a Political Weapon in
                     America.* New York: Oxford
                     University Press, 2007.

Laura K.   *The Cost of Counterterrorism: Power,
Donohue   Politics, and Liberty.* New York:
                     Cambridge University Press, 2008.

Anne Proffitt Dupree — *Speaking Up: The Unintended Costs of Free Speech in Public Schools.* Cambridge, MA: Harvard University Press, 2008.

Jon B. Gould — *Speak No Evil: The Triumph of Hate Speech Regulation.* Chicago, IL: Chicago University Press, 2005.

D.G. Hart — *A Secular Faith: Why Christianity Favors the Separation of Church and State.* Chicago, IL: Ivan R. Dee, 2006.

David Kuo — *Tempting Faith: An Inside Story of Political Seduction.* New York: Free Press, 2007.

Anthony Lewis — *Freedom for the Thought We Hate: A Biography of the First Amendment.* New York: Basic Books, 2008.

Jeremy Lipschultz — *Broadcast and Internet Indecency: Defining Free Speech.* New York: Routledge/Taylor and Francis Group, 2008.

Michelle Malkin — *In Defense of Internment: The World War II Round Up and What It Means for America's War on Terror.* Washington, DC: Regnery Publishing, 2004.

Andrew P. Napolitano — *A Nation of Sheep.* Nashville, TN: Thomas Nelson, 2007.

Martha Nussbaum — *Liberty of Conscience: In Defense of America's Tradition of Religious Equality.* New York: Basic Books, 2008.

John Durham
Peters

Courting the Abyss: Free Speech and the Liberal Tradition. Chicago, IL: Chicago University Press.

Erik Ringmar

A Blogger's Manifesto: Free Speech and Censorship in the Age of the Internet. New York: Anthem Press, 2007.

Anthony D. Romero and Dina Temple-Raston

In Defense of Our America: The Fight for Civil Liberties in the Age of Terror. New York: William Morrow, 2007.

Tara Ross and Joseph C. Smith Jr.

Under God: George Washington and the Question of Church and State. Dallas, TX: Spence Publishing, 2008.

James B. Rule

Privacy in Peril: How We Are Sacrificing a Fundamental Right in Exchange for Security and Convenience. New York: Oxford University Press, 2007.

Daniel J. Solove

Understanding Privacy. Cambridge, MA: Harvard University Press, 2008.

Amy E. White

Virtually Obscene: The Case for an Uncensored Internet. Jefferson, NC: McFarland & Co., 2006.

John K. Wilson

Patriotic Correctness: Academic Freedom and Its Enemies. Boulder, CO: Paradigm Publishers, 2008.

Robert Wuthnow

Saving America?: Faith-Based Services and the Future of Civil Society. Princeton, NJ: Princeton University Press, 2004.

Index